Trade Show Leads To Sales

Jeff Grundy

Copyright Information Page

ISBN-10: 1475036337
ISBN-13: 978-1475036336

Table of Contents

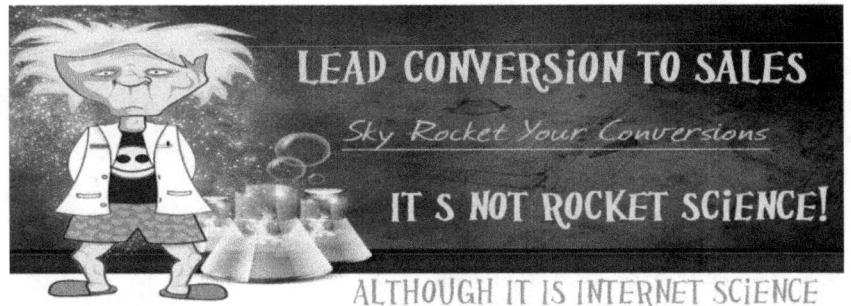

The ability to go online and see what others are saying about your product with a few simple clicks of the mouse has created a **complete game change**.

You now have a choice:

Let your prospects search the Internet and find **whatever** they happen to find about your company on their own.

Or

Position your company as an Industry Expert and let your prospects be wowed by your web presence.

This book is designed to give you a step by step process to build an online presence -- A presence which will leave no doubt in your prospect's mind that you are the trusted Authority in your Industry. It's time for the potential prospects to get to KNOW YOU, LIKE YOU and TRUST YOU.

Acknowledgments

Thank you

To my parents who through good times and tough times have always believed in me.

To my wife who married a Dreamer and who has suffered through all the years of tomorrow will be better.

To my daughter, who kept pushing me to keep dreaming.

To the infinite energy which has allowed me to piece together the ideas of the many authors mentioned in this book, into a system to put the fun back into growing a business.

Introduction

~~Facebook and Twitter are just not enough~~

In ancient internet times (and by ancient, I mean in the last 15-20 years), there was the website. Common understanding in business was that you must have a website, or else you couldn't survive. So everyone built websites, some spending tens of thousands of dollars. Then, the startling thing happened: no one came!

Next came Search Engine Optimization, otherwise known as SEO. The idea behind SEO was to optimize your site so that people can find you while doing searches on the internet. SEO included techniques such as on-page keyword optimization, meta tags, back-linking and a whole slew of other "musts" in order for your site to even consider competing in a competitive world of websites. New branches of marketing firms began popping up everywhere and SEO became the hottest new trend in website management. Their pitch: "Pay us truckloads of money and we will get you on the first page of Google."

As honest and rational this sounded, more times than not businesses would invest in SEO marketing firms only to see meager return to their website. But because everyone and anyone who managed a website insisted on SEO, money kept flowing to these firms and ROI became lost somewhere in the marketing budget.

It seemed as rapidly as the SEO industry grew, it gained a bad reputation just as quickly, largely due to a few unscrupulous companies. Actually as I am writing this I just received a call from a lady that offers business's help with their internet marketing. She started the conversation with "I stopped by your business the other day".

I work out of my home office (so I can watch my daughter grow up) and nobody drops by my business. I have no idea how you can start a sales presentation with a lie. Man, I HATE it when other people give my profession a bad reputation.

Sorry about the rant. Bottom line, ROI is sorely lacking when it comes to website creation and SEO. Now you could be reading this thinking "No way" our website generates tons of sales. Awesome, you are one of the few, consider yourself very fortunate. For the rest of you, read on.

Social Media Explosion

Over the last decade social media exploded at a blistering pace. Sites like LinkedIn, MySpace and even Friendster paved the way for the massive growth in this online social industry, but it wasn't until Facebook and Twitter appeared did consumers and businesses start to truly see the transformation and influence these social sites possessed over our culture and especially the purchasing power.

Simply put, if you are a business, big or small, the general consensus is you have to consider social media, such as Twitter and Facebook, if you want to survive in today's business world.

Yes, you still must have a website. Yes, you must do a certain amount of SEO. And yes, you must employ social media sites into your marketing and business mix. However, as I'll cover more in this book, these are techniques, not a be the-end-all and magically "poof" you have more sales or traffic.

Treat this new chapter in marketing like any other before it, with a plan. Whether it is SEO, social media or website creation, a proper plan aligning with your business' overall goals or purpose will get you further in the ROI race to the top.

This book is the better way

The book is divided into two parts. Part One is about creating the various web profiles, web properties and content needed to position your company as the trusted expert in your industry. Part Two outlines the 26-week follow up process and describes the media you should use to capitalizing your position as a trusted industry expert. Follow the tips and methodologies in this book and you'll enjoy seeing how easy it is to increase your percentage of Trade Show leads converted into SALES. Isn't it time the Internet starts providing some ROI?

Influence

Although I would love to take credit for the ideas in this book, very few of the ideas, if any, are mine. I am a strong believer in following the paths of successful people who have already done what I need to know.

As you will see throughout the book, I have taken the best information from the top experts in the fields I am utilizing. As we proceed through the process of creating your company as the industry expert, you will see ideas and examples from other authors. A few of the most notable are:

Dr Robert B, Cialdini, PH.D – Influence

Dan Kennedy – Direct Marketing

Chet Holmes – Sales

Jay Abrahams – Business Growth – Marketing

Frank Kern – Internet Marketing

Peter Guber – Story Telling

Let us begin with Dr. Cialdini and his book *Influence The Psychology of Persuasion* . Dr Cialdini breaks influence down into six Principles:

1. Reciprocation
2. Commitment and Consistency
3. Social Proof
4. Liking
5. Authority
6. Scarcity

The Trade Show ROI philosophy is based on Authority, Reciprocation and Social Proof.. We then incorporate Commitment and Consistency, Liking and Scarcity into the follow up sequence. The best way to get an overview of the principles is to watch Dr. Cialdini's six Youtube videos from a lecture he performed. You can see the videos at

http://TradeShowROI.org/influence-videos/

Authority

I don't think it is a surprise to anyone that Authority is an age-old principle of persuasion. We are told all our lives we must follow society's rules and obey our leaders. Why? Because of the power of Authority. It turns out if you are considered an expert in your field you are also considered an Authority. Cool, right? The question then becomes how can you utilize this principle to your benefit? The simple answer: acquire expert status in your industry and you automatically acquire influence over prospects seeking to do business with you.

Sure, you can spend six years or more in college or higher education, but in my observations the quickest way to become an expert in our society is to publish a book. Whether it is right or wrong, it does not matter. Throughout time we've associated experts with being published, because it is noble and scholarly. They must know their stuff and be an expert on the topic to write a whole book, right? This is how our minds work.

Often times I am seduced by this principle. When I visit a website, I often look to see if they have a book published or offered. If the answer is yes, I subconsciously think this is no average person. This person has Authority.

Becoming a published author is easier these days because of technology. In the past publishing a book would require a long writing and editing process, plus big negotiations with large publishing houses. Now with the arrival of Kindle, Nook and Create Space, anyone can publish a book. Better yet, these platforms not only publish your book but they will host it, market it, and even sell it to a massive audience.

Thus the core of our system is to instantly become a trusted authority by publishing your company's own book.

Reciprocation

Reciprocation is another age-old common life principle that is more and more used in marketing these days. In traditional marketing, it used to be a one-way message: business to consumer. It's like the saying goes, "give and ye shall receive." Give your prospects something, and you'll get something in return.

A simple technique to employ is to offer free, downloadable informational white papers, eBooks, statistical studies and just about anything you think your prospects would find useful related to your business. In turn, they fill more obliged to give you their email address or telephone number.

This is why it is a good idea to reciprocate comments or feedback made to your website. You don't have to reply to every single one, but by simply acknowledging the meaningful ones, potential prospects will view your company in a more favorably. In return, your company benefits from positive social proof, which brings us to our third concept.

Social Proof

In our fast moving technological, mobile and social world, Social Proof can make or break a business. It's the game changer.

You can spend hundreds of thousands of dollars on fancy high gloss brochures, white papers, or other traditional marketing materials, but it will mean nothing if your business lacks a compelling online presence. For instance, imagine you received a brochure for a traveling company in the mail. Intrigued by the professional-looking brochure, you decide to look up more about this company and go online. Low and behold, you find a sub-par website, an empty Facebook page, a totally spammed Twitter account and a few negative comments on some forum site. How has your opinion changed about the company?

In social proof, you cannot control what a prospect says and learns about your company, but there are ways to control that influence. This is often translated into sentiment of your company.

Surviving in today's social environment needs to be proactive, well thought out and consistent. Being a relatively new concept in the world of social marketing, few companies know how to exploit social proof very well. This is good news, because it evens the playing field. As other businesses struggle, your efforts will be greatly enhanced as the competition lags behind.

Social Proof for a company is about staying relevant, engaged and being ready to adapt to your audience and the fast changing trends in social media. A great example is Facebook's new timeline format. The ink may not be dry on the check you just wrote to your freelance developer or marketing firm to have your Facebook images and applications all designed, created and implemented and you wake up to find out Facebook has changed the format. Just when you had it all figured out, the platform changes.

If you are going to sit on the sidelines and wait until everything is settled and formalized on the internet before you get started, maybe you should be playing a different game, or better yet, in this day and age, get out of the game all together.

As a formally trained chef, the greatest example of social proof for me is recipes on the internet. Do a search for a recipe and what you find are dozens of websites featuring that one recipe or in some variation. Often times the recipes are written horribly, but that could just because of my trained culinary background. Nevertheless, social proof comes into play in the form of ratings and comments – a feedback loop. The more people try the recipe, rate and comment, the more sentiment weight is given. If positive, the recipe can be tweeted, blogged and reposted, thus extending the life of that piece of information. This is social proof at its best.

Now imagine if that was your company, your product, your service they were talking about.

(Just an aside, incorrect recipes are not always the authors fault. I had a full page recipe and picture of a banana cream pie in Food and Wine magazine and, somewhere between me submitting the recipe and it being printed, the recipe was changed. I have no idea how many people tried that recipe --the picture was awesome-- and were greatly disappointed with the results.)

Another example of building social proof is through prospecting, whether online or in-person. Say, for instance, you are at a trade show where nearly everyone who stops by your booth show genuine interest in your product or service. You have a good conversation with them, get them to sign up for a newsletter thus capturing their contact info and in turn you give them a brochure for them to check out later. Things all go well and then there's the follow-up.

The prospects barely remember your name, let alone what they spoke to you about at the trade-show, but you send them an email reminding them. Hopefully their interests are sparked again, intriguing them enough to go online to learn more about your product or service. This can go one of three ways:

Result 1

Your company website appears near the top of the search results page. The prospect clicks to enter your site, which is full of information about your company and what you do. However, it looks like the other couple dozen websites the prospect has seen on this same topic.. Click. Prospect is gone.

Result 2

Same as Result 1, but before clicking off the prospect sees a link to a Facebook page. "Cool," they think and then clicks over to view your Facebook page. Unfortunately, what the prospect is greeted with is a company page that has very few posts, low Like count, and no interaction. The most a person would get out of the page is to learn about your company and what you do, which she already gathered from visiting your website. Click. Prospect is gone.

Result 3

She can't believe her eyes. You company name is referenced in so many search page results that it would be difficult not to imaging the prospect saying, ""Wow, these guys must be good. They are everywhere." Along with your official company website, the prospect has a wide range of videos, forum boards, news or blog posts, pages, company listings and so on referencing your company. Even competitors are referencing your company's product, service or reputation. Now your prospect is thinking, "I know ABC corp they are one of the bigger players in our industry, if they like *your company* they must be good". Click. Prospect is off to find more information about YOU. Now the next time you send an email to your prospect, your chances of not being lost in the inbox black hole is greater.

As I've demonstrated, the obvious difference between Result 1 to Result 3 is the amount of chatter there is about your company online. It's the Social Proof that you need to get your business moving in a positive direction.

As consumers, we are often jaded by sales pitches and rarely believe the claims and documentation of from salespeople. In *Predictably Irrational* by Dan Ariely, a must read for any salesperson, the author discusses The Tragedy of the Commons, a theory which explains how a loss of Trust in others is slowly destroying society on the whole.

I am not a scholar, but it appears to me Social Proof is giving individuals a chance to fight back or take control. By being able to learn from multiple sources through comments, articles or forms of rating or ranking, we can again have faith in in what is being said is an honest statement. This is an extremely important concept and probably far above the scholarly level of this book. Yet, if true, means Social Proof is no fad, but indeed the glue needed to repair our lost trust for fellow man. My point being, Social Proof is only going to get more and more important culturally and within the consumer space, a possible reason for its incredibly fast growth

Lead Conversion and So Much More

Following is a brief overview of the Marketing System. This book focuses on taking raw leads and through the process of qualification, interaction and persuasion converting them to sales. By presenting the three parts of the marketing system, my hopes are you will on your own start to see how the social media will help you in every aspect of your Marketing.

Jay Abraham, known for creating over 6 billion dollars in revenue for his clients, says there are only three ways to grow your business:

Increase the number of customers who buy
Increase the average sales transaction value
Increase the number of times a customer buys

To achieve any of this, the marketing system must comprise of three techniques:

1. Marketing to Past Clients

2. Referrals

3. Sales System

As stated previously, this book is all about the sales system or increasing the number of customers who buy. The idea here is to not only apply your company's new expert status to lead conversions but also to referrals and past clients.

Now that you understand Authority, Reciprocity and Social Proof and have a strong web presence for your company, grab the marketing team and start brain storming the new possibilities to make the sales marketing system work. Building a good pool of ideas to strategize from and put your company in the position to turn raving fans into increased transactions.

Here are some examples:

Special skype group for customers

Monthly Facebook giveaway for current customers

Special webinars to inform and upsell current clients

Tips and tricks blogs to help increase productive and lower cost of your product

Q&A day once a month to keep customers connected

Guest post on your bog to keep customer involved (others will want to see what competition is doing)

Public referral contest on social media site (give away a cruise – get 10 customers?)

Joint ventures with customers via your sites.

Flat out ask for referrals via your sites.

Scavenger hunt at your factory and promote via social sites.

Before we move on I would like to talk about one more point Jay Abraham is also know for and that is the concept of building pillars (individual strategies) of business growth, The idea is that growth occurs exponentially each time a new pillar is added.

For example, using basic made up numbers, let's say you have a webinar by itself and it converts 3 viewers into strong qualified prospects. You also have a book and it converts 3 readers out of 100 into strong prospects. So individually each acquires 3 for a total of 6 prospects.

Now lets say in the webinar you mention the book and in the book your mention the webinar. Now you find that several of the readers who were not moved after watching the webinar but who then read the book become prospects. So now the book produced 5 qualified prospects. The same happens with the book who then watch the webinar and it now is producing 5 prospects.

Hopefully I have not completely confused you, but essentially by themselves, the webinar and book created a total of 6 qualified prospects. However, when used together they produced 10 prospects.

Now raise your pillars of social properties to 10. Instead of generating 30 leads (10 sites *3 leads) you are now generating 100 or 150 qualified leads. Social Media itself has added to this as most users of the internet just naturally go from one web property to another.

Preparation

Alice :   Would you tell me, please, which way
I ought to go from here?
The Chesire Cat: That depends a good deal on where you
want to get to
Alice: I don't much care where.
The Cat: Then it doesn't much matter which way you
go.

> By Lewis Carroll – *Alice in Wonderland*

The best part about being an author is you can put whatever you want
in the book and I have always wanted to put this quote in one of my
books. As you continue on in this adventure with me, begin to think
about what should be written in your own company book. . Just
remember the book does not, and probably should not, be done in
house. You can inexpensively have a book created these days. We will
discuss this in detail later, for now keep thinking what you would write
to get your prospects to Know, Like and Trust You.

Back to the quote. It is certainly a well-used cliché, but loaded with
truth. It is crazy to spend hundreds of hours or pay someone
thousands of dollars to create a massive web presence for your
company, without knowing what you are trying to accomplish.
Examples may include:

- Branding
- Increasing lead conversion
- Creating traffic to your company website
- Selling from your website
- Pre-selling from your website
- Directing all the traffic to a webinar

- Creating a relationship with your prospects
- Qualifying your prospects
- Educating your prospects

That is not to say you cannot do more than one. Yet a website that is trying to sell a product looks far different from a website trying to direct the prospect to an educational webinar. I am not advocating creating a committee and taking six months to draw up a proposal, but taking a day to prioritize your actions, related to your desired outcomes so your money is wisely spent. Also it will be just plain more effective.

Next, you need to know who is doing the searching. This can become a pretty complex issue and several recent books have gone into great detail. Google "customer persona" for more detailed explanations on this topic. If anything, it'll give you a good starting point on who are your current customers or potential prospects.

You can see a quick 4 minute overview on personas on the video page here

http://tradeshowroi.org/influence-videos/

Basically, you want to figure out everything you can about your prospect; not only who they are, but what are their interests and what they want. More importantly, it helps to understand how effectively to communicate to various prospect groups. People falling into specific age groups, ethnicities, gender or other social affiliations communicate and respond differently. One thing to remember when creating a customer persona is that it a real-life person or current customer. Rather a customer persona is a representation or characterization of who are your current customers or prospects, using combined psychographic and demographic data already collected by your company.

A great tactic is to give your persona a name and an image. Now direct your writing to the individual persona you have created. Your content will now become much more compelling to the reader.

As the prospect moves through the follow up process, you may have several different personas that you can assign them to, becoming even more specific in your type of media and content.

Keywords

Simply put a keyword is the word or phrase someone types into a search engine (Google 60+% of the time) when they are searching for information. Keep in mind social media sites also act as search-engines, meaning YouTube, Twitter, Facebook, etc. all work on the same principle. You enter a keyword and they return relevant results. The important word here is relevant. Google owns the search market because at present their searches are the most relevant to the searchers needs.

Google bases it results on algorithms. The algorithms are never made public but many have tried to reverse engineer them in order to try and trick Google into placing their sites higher in the Search-Engine Results. Search-Engine Optimization (SEO) is founded on this idea.

Google is pretty smart, well more like extremely smart. As new loopoles are discovered by marketers and developers Google changes their search algorithms. This is largely so that people cannot game the system and monopolize the top spots in search engine results.. From on page optimization to off page optimization, from article marketing to back linking, trying to get on the first page of Google has been a constantly changing process.

The great news is, with the massive explosion of Social Media, SEO is becoming simpler. The latest updates from Google now take into account, tweets from Twitter, Facebook posts, bookmarking sites, what you say in your Gmails (yes big brother is watching), Google+, YouTube and on and on. It no longer takes SEO tricks; it just takes having great content people are talking about.

You'd think that the title of this section should be called Google, rather than Keywords. , It's not so, only because keywords, Google and Social Media are all importantly related to one another. You want to make sure the keywords you are spending time and money on are actual terms that people are looking for. This means using keyword tools to optimize your social pages, websites, videos, comments – everything – with strong keywords.

How do you go about starting a process like this? Say you are looking to promote a website on *Lampropeltis triangulum sinaloae.* You can put up a hundred sites and post about it every day, but it will do you absolutely no good if nobody is looking for *Lampropeltis triangulum sinaloae* or talking about them. Yet according to Google's keyword research tool 40,500 people globally search for milk snakes a month. Quite a difference 40,500 or 0 when both are searching for the exact same thing. To increase your chance for exposure, think of other keywords that are associated with your main topic, like "snake" or "small snake."

You can find the keyword tool at *https://adwords.**google**.com/select/**Keyword**ToolExternal* or just search Google for Google keyword tool.

The Book

"They are a self-serving, monopolizing, difficult to enter, old boys club. Thanks."

- As quoted by me.

Some may disagree, but I bet plenty vigorously nod their head in agreement to the statement above. As I have stated earlier, in the past it has been very difficult to get a book published. If I recall correctly, the most famous example would be the authors of *Chicken Soup for the Soul*, Jack Canfeld and Mark Victor Hansen who were turned down 140 times. Say it again, 140 times! Today, it has now sold over 112 million copies. Even the famous civil war story-turned all-time classic *Gone with the Wind,* was turned down down 30 times.

But I digress. The point is, right or wrong, publishing a book can be a difficult and expensive process creating the aura or prestige of a published author. When it comes to nonfiction, it is an Expert Aura.

Certainly there are other reasons a book in our society gives the author instant expert credibility. But who cares what the reason is, it is still possible to take advantage of publishing a book. Besides the book being a great way to educate your prospect, it is more importantly creating trust and like with your prospects.

Tests have shown over and over we believe what we read more than what we hear. More importantly, the prospect is not only reading your words, they are saying them out loud in their mind. They are not just listening to your sales presentation; they are saying it in their own mind in their own voice.

You may remember hearing this in school (back in the day for many of us), that finding your voice is extremely important to writing. Discovering and fostering your own personal writing style allows reader, and in this case, prospects to get to know you and trust you.

During my catering career I did a special event for a jewelry store. For many years prior I had become familiar with hearing the owners voices through radio commercials.   So when I went to meet with them to pick the menu, the sound of their voices made me think we were old friends. The same will hold true for a book.

The readers will believe they know your company on a personal level. A prospect will frame any future discussion with you or your company as a personal and professional advisory role rather than a salesperson.

Framing Your Book

Framing your book is about how to communicate your message through tone and literary persuasiveness. In general terms, it is also about changing the way you look at something depending on how the current situation has been presented to you in the past.

Recently I attended a chorus performance for my daughter. (She was picked the #1 singer in her school by a panel of judges – proud dad :)). As part of the presentation they had an introduction by a group of barbershop singers. They sang their first song and I was impressed, yet I wanted to see my daughter sing. Then the group leader introduced them and mentioned at the World Competition in Arizona in 2011 they took 2nd place.

Now all the sudden I was not being interrupted by a group of singers, I was completely engaged in watching every move and listening to every sound of the #2 best barbershop singers in the world.

Here's another example. Studies show that if you go into a restaurant and see two prices for meals, one priced at $10 and the other at $5, chances are you are more likely to pick the cheaper of the two meals. Now if the choices are increased and there are three meals priced at $12, $10 and $5, statistics show that you are more likely to choose the $10 meal. It's not so much the actual price, but the way it was framed that makes this example. The $10 meal doesn't look as expensive anymore.

If you have not guessed already the whole idea of Trade Show ROI is to re-frame the way your prospects look at your company. The idea is to change their view of your company from just another company to the Industry Expert. Once this is done, purchasing from you becomes almost a natural response by prospects. They are compelled to buy from you since you are the expert.

And yes, a book is the easiest most effect way to re-frame your prospect view of your company. Pretty cool stuff, right?

Better yet, with advancement of self-publishing technology and on demand publishing, the process is now very cost effective. Once the transcript for your book is created and properly formatted, electronic versions of the book can be available the same day on websites such as Amazon (Kindle) and Barnes and Noble (Nook).

On demand publishing means that no inventory is created. The book is not produced until it is sold.
This eliminates the need to invest in buying 5,000 physical books or even the cost of storage. With Create Space, not only will they on demand publish the book, but they also help with the distribution and marketing.

As we will discuss several more times through this book, content creation is simple. It's as simple as asking every employee in your company, from parking attendant to CEO, to write three to five paragraphs about the benefits of your product or service and you are on your way to building content for your book.

If you need more ideas, here are some simple tips for writing your book:

- Have someone else do it. It will get done that way. It is much easier to edit a book then write one from scratch,
- It does not have to be 30,000 words. Don't make it a white paper but it does not have to be a novel
- Use the same writing style as your prospects. This can be serious, technical, funny, conversational, etc.
- Make it Interesting, lots of quotes and maybe some pictures
- It is not a sales pitch. No Sales
- Include Links to your website and other social media properties
- Mention your competition
- Have a good book cover. Only 3% of purchasers are said to read a book anyways

Tips for submitting book to Digital Publishers

- Title is keyword rich
- Cover looks professional
- Description describes Industry
- Proper category
- Accepted formatting
- Real reviews
- Acceptable amount of advertising

YouTube

I love YouTube. I am not a major TV fan, but I do love movies, plus I don't read very much (I listen to as many books as I can via audible.com). So maybe that makes sense why I like watching videos. I am also a prime prospect in this medium.

Give a person a 5 page article on *Lampropeltis triangulum sinaloae* or a five minute video. Which one do you think this person will choose?

I have been hearing for over a year now that YouTube was the second largest search engine, maybe Facebook is now, let's just say top three. But until recently, I could never understand why. After my first search I was hooked. Looking for Lampropeltis *triangulum sinaloae* not only will you find it, you will find a video of it eating a mouse. My point is you can find whatever you want on YouTube, plus most of the time you see it in action.

For businesses, this means having a presence on YouTube is ever more important in the world of Authority and Social Proof. The ability to not only research an author, but to be able to actually watch parts of a lecture is so beneficial to understanding their message or their topic of expertise.

The key to making this cost effective is not shooting a full-fledged TV quality commercial. The whole video can be shot on a good quality phone, or flip camera which costs about $100 and directly downloads to your computer. The actual flip camera software will even post the video to YouTube for you.

Let me repeat this. You do not need a professional quality video, no one expects it. A little bit of shaking and wind noise just adds to its authenticity.

Many videos do not even need to be a video. A screen capture of a power point presentation is one of the most common forms of videos.

Mike Koenigs of Traffic Geyser software is probably the Internet's most knowledgeable person on web traffic and videos. He recommends doing a 10 video series. He suggests finding out the 10 biggest objections your salespeople are presented with and then doing a short 3 minute or so power point type video answering the objections.

You can see a video of Mike describing video marketing at

http://tradeshowroi.org/influence-videos/

The video is more about Internet Marketing but it is a good overview.

YouTube is also a powerful tool for discovery as well. Using keywords you can optimize your video meta data to appear in the related videos section of a similar video. Imagine that a potential prospect is watching one of your competitor's videos if they even have one. Because you took the time to optimize your videos, many of your videos show in the related videos section of your competitor's page, tempting the prospect to move away from your competitor and onto you.

Adding a call to action at the end of the video and in the provided caption moves your prospect several steps closer to a purchase.

Did I say Google loves YouTube also? So much so they bought them.

Tips for creating videos:

- Keep them as short as possible. 20 minute videos can work but 3 and 4 minute videos are best
- Put your company URL first in the Description
- Keywords in Title
- Keywords and Compelling copy in description
- Call to Action
- Make the videos fun if possible
- Keep it simple
- Create a YouTube Channel
- Ask viewer to subscribe to your channel

Keep in mind the videos by themselves have little value. It doesn't matter how good and compelling your videos is if no one views them, they are worthless. From my observations, the vast numbers of instructional videos and training videos on YouTube have fewer than 50 views. Check it out for yourself. In order to be fully effective, your overall marketing strategy must have a way of pushing prospect to your videos.

Content

You read about it all the time, **Content is King**. This has been true for vary degrees throughout the Internet's history. With the explosion of Social Media this has never been so true. With thousands of other choices available to prospects, your content must be compelling enough to keep their trigger happy finger from clicking away from you and never returning. Your content must be engaging and interesting enough to get the reader to follow your desired calls to action.

As we have seen, content comes in many different modes and is distributed across many different types of media. Combine this with different types of content (i.e. books, blog posts, videos) to the different personas, it is understandable you may may feel overwhelmed.

It is no surprise that people who start blogs and other social media ventures end up giving up on the process fairly quickly or pass off the assignment to someone who has no idea what they are doing.

The first step ensuring compelling content is, like I've mentioned several times already: preparation and planning. Compile the content and organize into categories or interesting buckets

Here are some helpful tips to get you and your company started on content creation:

- Tape talks or presentations at company events and have them transcribed
- Tape you salespeople's presentations and having them transcribed
- Utilize your training materials, digitalize them and offer for free content
- Find information others are writing about you
- Quote others in your industry
- Get customers feedback and display as testimonials

- ⅄ Hire ghostwriters

- ⅄ Have a contest among employees to write the company story

- ⅄ Read books on telling stories. (Tell to Win - The Writers Journey: Mythic Structure for Writers)

- ⅄ Collect comments from your social media sites

- ⅄ Post surveys and answers to polls Inter office emails

- ⅄ Encourage people to record content how they like to. Meaning if people like to talk let them speak it into a recorder then transcribe

A great tip from *Managing Content Marketing* by Robert Rose is to storyboard your idea, then create a story from the pictures. You can even input the pictures directly into Pinterest, or create a power point for SlideShare.

Speaking of *Managing Content Marketing,* there is a great section in the book on Editorial Guidelines to create a framework for you content. Basically before you begin writing, develop a set of rules (limited – not overwhelming to inhibit process) so you know what and what you cannot write about.

When writing your content focus on making it:

- ⅄ Informative not sales

- ⅄ Compelling copy with calls to action

- ⅄ Re-purpose (blogs, videos,tweets,slide presentations, webinars)

- ⅄ Mix with interactive games, quizzes, polls

- ⅄ Fresh

- ⅄ Continuous

- ⅄ Consistent

Remember, content is just not the written posts on Facebook or Twitter, or images you post to Pineterst or Flickr. It has to have meaning and purpose, which ultimately drives traffic back to your business.

Also important to note is to be careful in your selection of your images. First for copyright and legal issues and secondly to keep it consistent throughout all your web properties or traditional marketing material..

On social sites, filling in your profiles 'about' and 'information' areas are the most important part of setting up a social media site. The description must draw the prospect to take some type of action. Descriptions and titles should also be keyword oriented and driving the prospect in one direction.

Re-purposing is your best friend. Find out which content is getting the most feedback and convert it into all your other media. A video can easily be transcribed into a post. A great post can be turned into a PowerPoint presentation. Do you have a webinar that is getting awesome reviews? Turn it into a series of 10 posts. Take your book and make a video series out of the 20 most important points.

Creating a game plan for your content will increase the odds you will continue providing information.

"The best laid plans of mice and men"

- Of Mice and Men ,JohnSteinbeck

Deciding to create an Expert Status on the Internet, creating multi web properties, using a follow up marketing system are all good but basically worthless unless you produce consistent content. It is easy to say I will make 10 posts a day across the various web properties, and you will for a week or so, then business gets in the way. The easiest and most productive way to accomplish your goal is to create a schedule and follow it.

Pick the method you are most likely to follow, day timer, PDA, phone software, pc program and create a schedule for how many posts you will make a day on what property using what media. Now stick to it, and if you can't stick to it hire a company that can stick to it for you.

I realize that content is the key to making the whole system work and I have devoted very little space to it. It truly deserves a complete book by itself. Dozens of books have been written, my favorite is *Managing Content Marketing* by Robert Rose & Joe Pulizzi

Web Presence

My original idea for this book was to list each web property, give an overview and then include detailed instructions on how to sign up. With new social sites and trends changing nearly every day, this seemed like a bad idea.

Then I recently signed up for a service, which was to convert this book into a Kindle format since doing it manually is a real challenge. From a programmer's or more technically savvy person, unlike myself, the software seemed pretty straight forward, thus they did not provide any documentation on how to use it. Unfortunately for me, I was pretty frustrated, wasting over an hour trying to figure out what to do.

Using this experience as a lesson, I am going to include the basic sign up information for those readers who want it. Please remember that some of the information will become obsolete almost as soon as I publish it. Yet I believe it will give a good overview and you can always visit the individual site for updated information.

If you know the information just skip to the next section of the book, although some of the newer sites such as Pinterest may be helpful. There is also an explanation of four different RSS platforms you may find educational.

Facebook Pages

Facebook is by far the largest social media platform in the world. Creating a page on Facebook's platform allows you to reach millions of new people, as well as stay in touch with existing fans. Viral pages have been known to reach hundreds of thousands of people in as quickly as a week from creation.
Here's how to create a Facebook Page, as well as a few tips for success.

Step 1: Getting Started

Get started by going to http://www.facebook.com/pages/. Click on "Create Page."

| My Pages · Pages I Admin · | Poland | ⟶ | + Create Page |

Step 2: Choose Page Type

Select what kind of page you want to create.

Step 3: Name Your Page

Give your page a name. If Facebook needs additional basic information, they'll ask for it here.

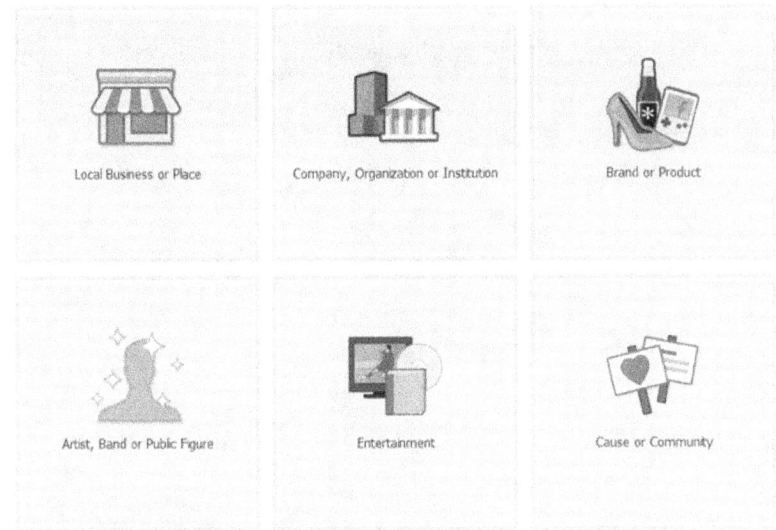

Local Business or Place   Company, Organization or Institution   Brand or Product

Artist, Band or Public Figure   Entertainment   Cause or Community

Step 3: Name Your Page

Give your page a name. If Facebook needs additional basic information, they'll ask for it here.

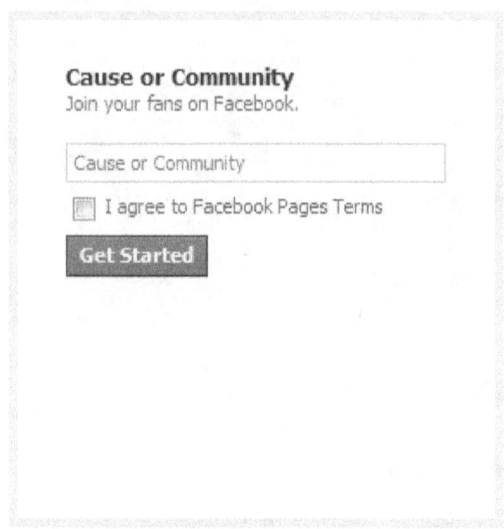

Step 4: Add Profile Image

Add an image from either your website or from your computer. Pick an image that accurately represents your brand.

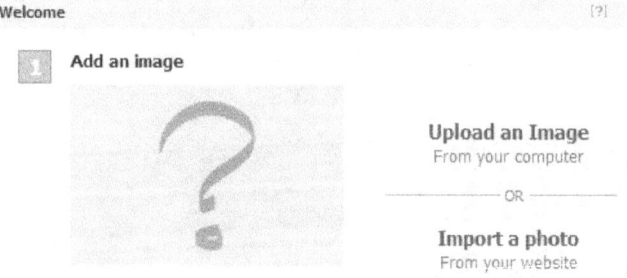

Step 5: Invite People

Once your page is up, it's time to get people to visit. There are two ways you can do this: By building friends, or by importing your contact list from somewhere else. The first option will send a Facebook invite, while the second will take your existing contacts and let them know you've created a page.

2 **Invite your friends**

Start building your fan base by suggesting this Page to friends who might like it.

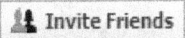

3 **Tell your fans**

Let your current customers and subscribers know about your new Page.

Step 6: Add a Like Box

Another way to get more people to your page is to add a like box to your website. Just click the "Add Like Box" button, select how you want your box to look and paste the code onto your website.

5 **Promote this Page on your website**

Add a Facebook Like Box to your site and give people an easy way to discover and follow this Page.

Add Like Box

You can choose the width and height of the box, the overall color, whether or not you want faces showing, whether or not you want a stream showing and more.

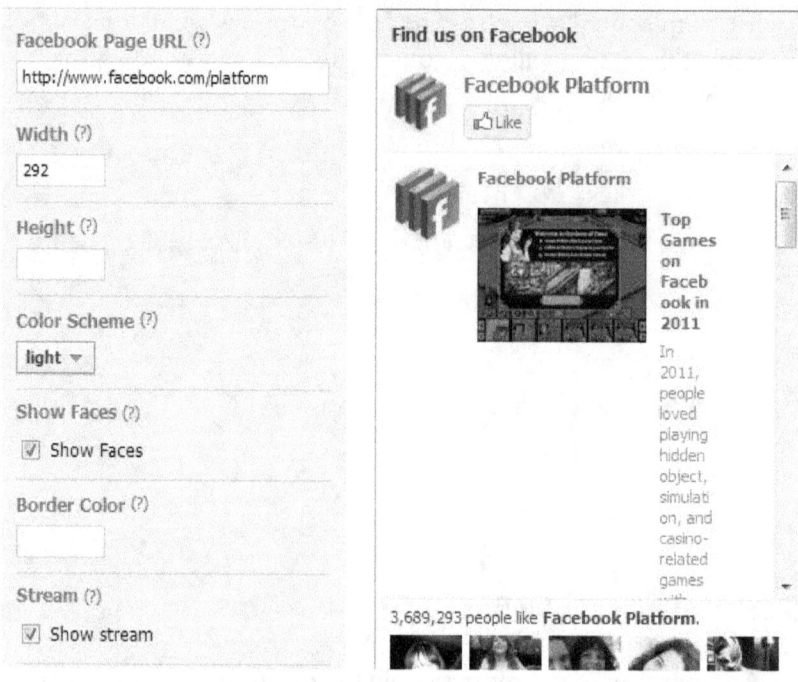

Step 7: Edit Your Information

Click the "Edit Info" button at the top to edit your page details.

Edit your category and most importantly your description. You can also create a username for your page here.

Category:	Other Community [?]
Official Page:	Pick a topic [?]
Username:	Create a username for this page? Learn more.
Name:	Example Page
About:	
Description:	
Website:	Website

Save Changes   Close

Step 8: Posting to the Wall

All that's left is to post content to your wall. Posting to your wall is like posting to any other wall on Facebook. You can post in text, as well as attach multimedia content and hyperlinks. One unique feature of pages is the ability to ask questions.

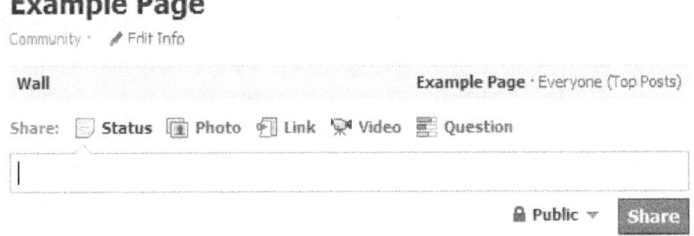

Tips for Running a Successful Facebook Page

Here are a few tips for running a successful Facebook page.

- Short, Snappy Posts. People on Facebook will usually see you content through their feeds, rather than explicitly visiting your page. When you're appearing in their feeds, it's best to have short and snappy posts. This helps catch their attention and keep it. Overly long or boring posts tend to lose readership.
- Post Regularly. Get people used to reading your content. Try to post on a regular schedule, daily if possible. Since a status update really shouldn't take more than 5 minutes to write, you can even write it all at once for the week and just post it at the end of the day every day.
- Have a Two-Way Dialogue. Get your readership involved. Ask them questions. Have conversations. Don't just use your page as a one way outlet of information and promotions. Instead, use your page to actually talk to your customers. Give them a chance to express themselves.
- Encourage Free Speech. One of the biggest mistakes brands make is limiting what customers can and can't say. Even if customers are posting dissident information on your boards, you should welcome the opposition. Let your readers speak freely.
- Respond. If you don't respond regularly and quickly to comments and questions, people will simply stop responding. On the other hand, if you respond quickly and regularly, people will enjoy participating more and do it more regularly.
- Use Multimedia. Don't just use text. A few years ago, communicating through social media with just text was entertaining and engaging. Today however, to really catch someone's attention you should use a variety of media, including images and videos.
- Be Human. Don't just be an anonymous brand. Let them get to

know you, who you are, what you stand for and your personality. Don't be afraid to make a joke or let a little humanity come through.

- ▲ Give Value. Every once in a while, host a contest or giveaway that's exclusive to your Facebook fans. This helps create reciprocity and increases loyalty. Reward them for following you on Facebook.

Twitter

Twitter allows business owners to interact with customers in a very unique, spontaneous and quick way. With Twitter, you can market to other business owners as often as you'd like. If you "spammed" Facebook status updates or email messages, you'd get penalized. On Twitter however, you could make a new post every hour and be commended for it.

Here's how to use Twitter for business.

Step 1: Create a New Account

To create a new account, go to http://www.Twitter.com. Fill out the new account form.

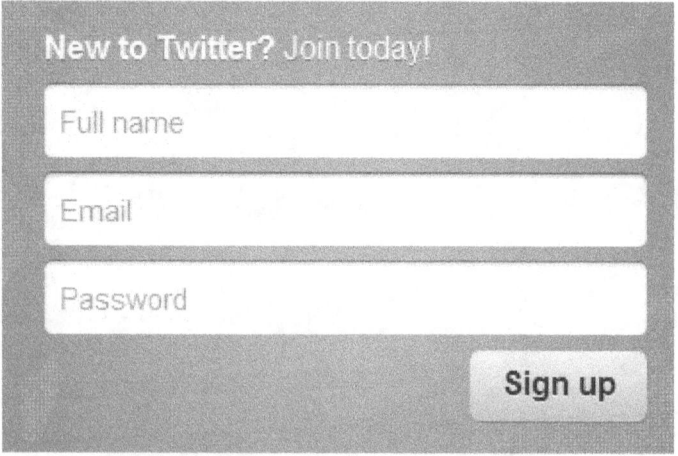

Step 2: Startup Wizard

Go through the startup wizard if it's your first time using Twitter. You'll be invited to add people based on categories.

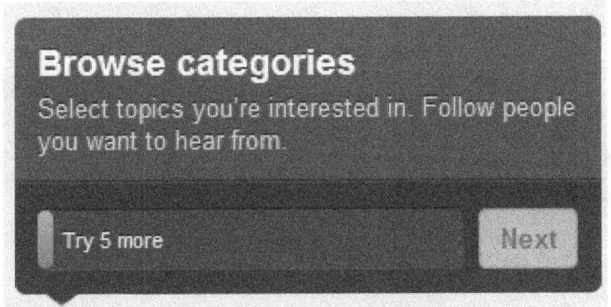

You'll also be invited to search for and add contacts based on your email.

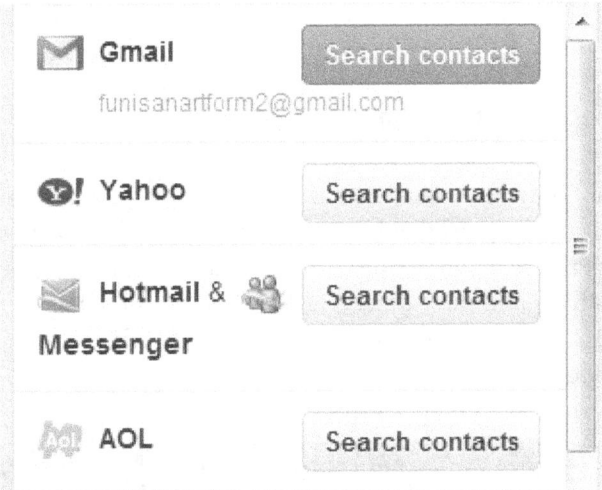

Use the categories feature and the search contacts feature to populate your initial follow list.

Step 3: Posting New Tweets

To post a Tweet to anyone who's following you, type your message into the box on the left. Twitter limits tweets to 140 characters. This will be sent out to all your followers.

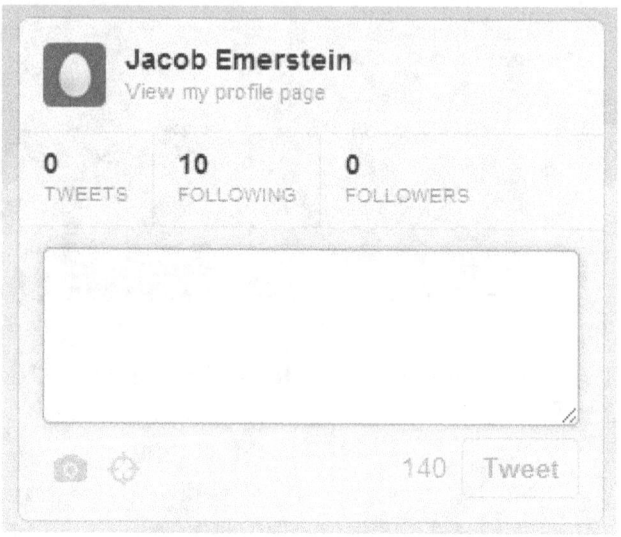

Step 4: See Who's Talking to You

When someone wants to talk to you on Twitter, what they do is use a mention. They do this by putting the @ symbol in front of your name. For example, if your username was Jacob123, they would tweet something and put @Jacob123 in the beginning.

To see who's been talking about you with this feature, just go to @ Connect along the top.

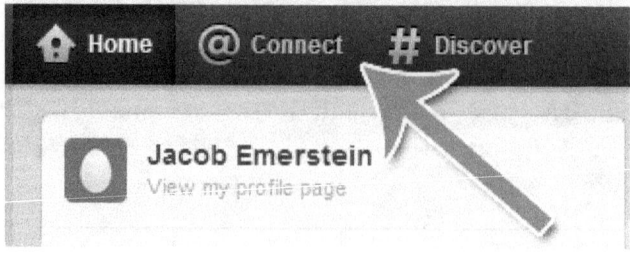

Note: If you and another tweeter are mutually following one another, you can communicate with direct messages. Otherwise, you have to use @ connects.

Step 5: Discover More People to Follow

To discover more people to follow, just click "Discover" along the top navigation bar. You can browse by category, by stories, by level of activity, by recommendations and by finding friends.

Step 6: Using the Feed

Once you've followed a handful of people, you'll be able to see their tweets in your feed. To reply to a tweet, retweet a tweet or favorite a tweet, just hover your mouse over the tweet and click the corresponding button.

Tweets

Gary Vaynerchuk @gar   ← Reply ⇄ Retweet ★ Favorite · Open
Thank god I am hungry instagr.am/p/b8vp6/
▣ View photo

Nick Jonas @nickjonas   57m
I hope everyone had an amazing Christmas!

FT **Financial Times** @FinancialTimes   6h
French unemployment at 12-year high on.ft.com/sXF2Vi
#FinancialTimes

Twitter Tips for Businesses

Using Twitter for business? Here are a few tips for building your readership and improving rapport with customers.

Use outside tools. Twitter's default interface is great for the casual user, but is missing many features for business users. For example, you can't schedule a tweet to be sent later. Use outside applications that add functionality to Twitter.

Pay attention to your avatar & background. Having an avatar and background that resonates with your brand can work wonders. The moment someone lands on your site, they should immediately "feel" like they're interacting with your brand.

Make it easy to follow you. Place a Twitter button on your main website, on your posts, on your pages and generally anywhere that people can find you.

Search for related keywords and answer questions. For example, if you run a Canada travel website, search for tweets like "going to Canada" or "flying to Toronto" and send people tips about the places they're going.

Use RT @name to retweet. The new retweet format won't get you noticed, because it lacks the @tweet inclusion. If you're retweeting something, make sure to use the "RT @name" format so you show up on their @ Connect tab.

Tweet regularly. Get people in the habit of seeing your content. The more often you tweet, the more your content will be exposed to people. On Twitter, it's very hard to tweet too often.

LinkedIn

LinkedIn is the one social network dedicated to connecting professionals with other professionals. Through LinkedIn, you can reach a completely different crowd of people than any other social network.

Using LinkedIn, you can find extremely high ticket customers. You can find potential investors willing to put in hundreds of thousands, even millions into funding your company. You can find potential business partners. You can find top notch talent to work in your company.

The list of ways to use LinkedIn for business goes on and on. Here's how to setup an account, along with a few tips for making the most of your LinkedIn experience.

Step 1: Create the Account

Go to http://www.LinkedIn.com to being the account creation process. Fill in your name, email and password to get started.

Join LinkedIn Today

First Name:

Last Name:

Email:

Password:

6 or more characters

Join Now *

Already on LinkedIn? Sign in.

On the next page you'll be asked for some basic information.

I live in: Poland ▼

Postal Code:

e.g. 00-001 (Only your region will be public, not your postal code)

I am currently: ⦿ Employed   ◯ Job Seeker   ◯ Student

Job title:

☐ I am self-employed

Company:

Create my profile

Click "Create my Profile" and your account will be created.

Step 2: Search for Contacts

If you want to import your contacts from your email account, you can do so here. Just give LinkedIn your login information and they'll use your address book to find everyone who you've sent emails or received emails from.

Searching your email contacts is the easiest way to find people you already know on LinkedIn.

Your email:	funisanartform@gmail.com
Email password:	

Continue

We will not store your password or email anyone without your permission.

Step 3: Add a Photo

Once you're in your profile, the first thing you should do is add a photo. Make sure the photo you add is professional and creates a good first impression. Click the "Add Photo" button in the picture frame to add your photo.

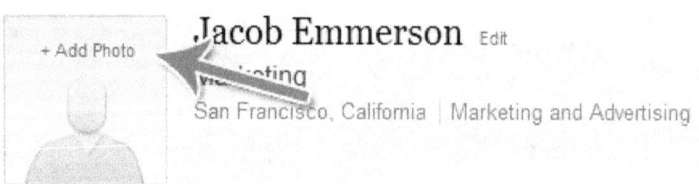

Jacob Emmerson Edit

San Francisco, California | Marketing and Advertising

Step 4: Add Details

Adding more details will help give you more credibility. It'll help prospective employers, investors, partners and clients get a sense of who you are. Add as much information as you can.

Click any of the links to bring up a more detailed "add information" screen.

Current	+ Add a current position
Past	+ Add a past position
Education	+ Add a school
Recommendations	+ Ask for a recommendation
Connections	+ Add connections
Websites	+ Add a website
Twitter	+ Add a Twitter account
Public Profile	http://www.linkedin.com/pub/jacob-emmerson/45/31a/a04 Edit

Each information section looks slightly different. Again, fill out each section with as much detail as you can. It's not unusual to spend two or three hours on LinkedIn just filling out profile information.

School Name:	
Degree:	
Field(s) of Study:	

Examples: English, Physics, Economics

Dates Attended: [- ▼] to [- ▼]

Tip: Current students: enter your expected graduation year

Activities and Societies:

Tip: Use commas to separate multiple activities
Examples: Alpha Phi Omega, Chamber Chorale, Debate Team

Additional Notes:

See examples

[Save Changes] or Cancel

Step 5: Contact Information

Give people a variety of different ways to contact you. Again, the more you can fill out the better. Some people prefer to pick up the phone and call you, while others will prefer to email you. Still others want to check out your Twitter first, before contacting you on instant message.

Additional Information

Websites: + Add

Twitter: + Add

Interests: + Add

Groups and   + Add
Associations:

Honors and Awards: + Add

Personal Information Edit

Phone: + Add

Address: + Add

IM: + Add

Birthday: + Add

Marital status: + Add

Step 6: Contact Preferences

Let LinkedIn know what you want to be contacted about. If you're just looking for clients, this will prevent employers from contacting you. If you're just looking for investors, this will prevent potential employees from contacting you.

Contact Jacob for: Change contact preferences

- career opportunities   • consulting offers
- new ventures   • job inquiries
- expertise requests   • business deals
- reference requests   • getting back in touch

Step 7: Add, Change or Manage Connections

Connections are the core of LinkedIn. If you want to succeed, you need to have a lot of connections. You need to keep your connections alive by contacting them every once in a while. You need to make sure that you add people who you meet at marketing meetings.
To check or add connections, go to the "Contacts" menu in the top navigation bar.

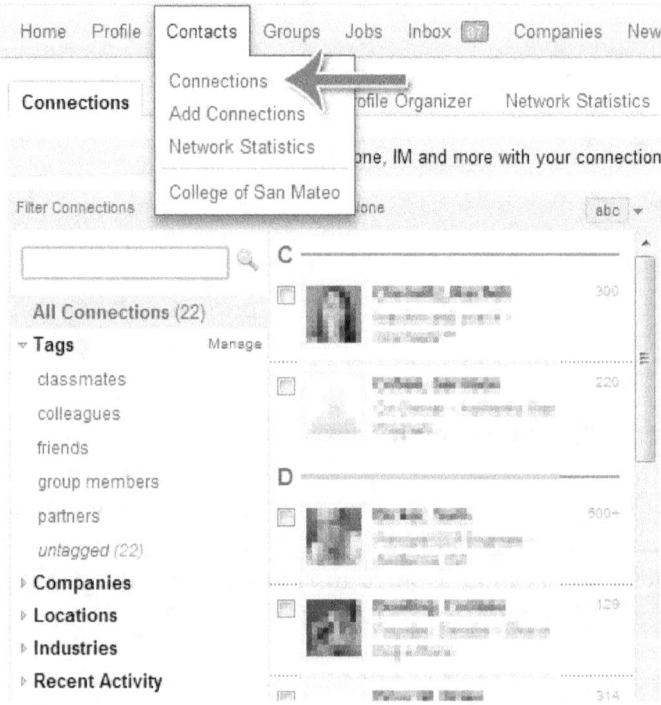

Step 8: Groups

Groups are one of the best ways to meet new people. Groups allow you to meet new people in your industry that you may not have had connections to before.

There are groups for just about everything. From manufacturing to internet marketing, from entry level to executive level. Groups can help you meet employees and employers, investors and clients.

To browse groups, see recommended groups, join a group or see what groups you're already a part of, use the "Groups" menu tab at the top.

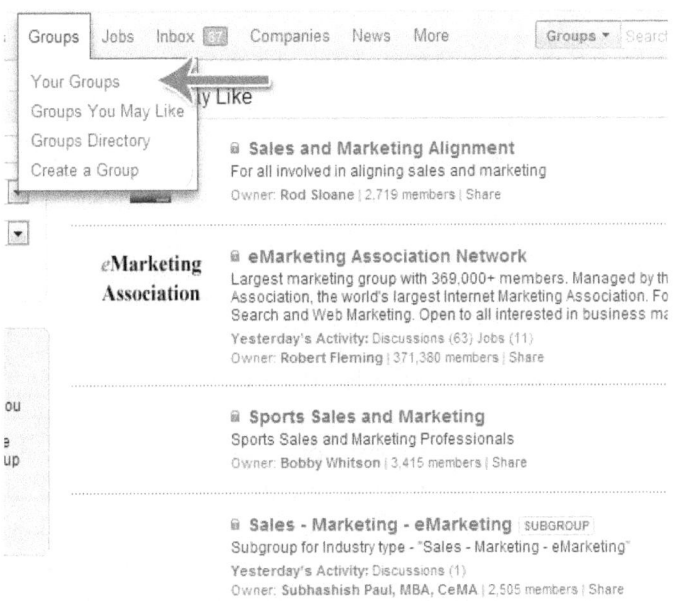

Step 9: Hire an Employee or Find a Job

LinkedIn has one of the most responsive job boards on the planet. Unlike other job advertising sites, the people who tend to respond to ads on LinkedIn tend to be highly qualified.

To post a job or find a job, use the "Jobs" tab along the top.

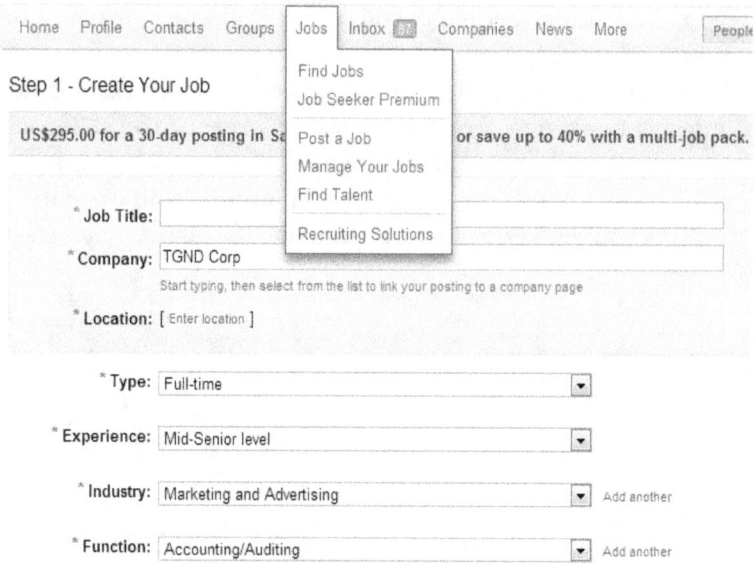

Tips for Using LinkedIn for Business

- ⋏ Here are a few tips for optimizing your LinkedIn profile, building trust and meeting the people you want to meet.
- ⋏ Ask previous employers, partners and co-workers to write recommendations for you. Having recommendations from people you've had professional relationships with can really boost your credibility.
- ⋏ Ask past clients to write recommendations. When a client writes a recommendation, it's visible to their entire social network. In other words, in addition to be an endorsement for you, you get instant visibility as well.
- ⋏ Proactively write recommendations. Write recommendations for clients, for suppliers, for employees, employers and everyone else. When you write someone a recommendation, there's a very good chance they'll write you one back. Give and

you shall receive. Best of all, writing a recommendation costs absolutely nothing.

- ⋏ Attend events where clients, employers or investors might be attending. LinkedIn gives you the ability to see which of the people you know are attending a certain event. This allows you to pick and choose events based on the people you want to "bump into" while you're there.
- ⋏ Use it to vet vendors and suppliers. Instead of having to take a vendor at their word about their product quality, you can find and use only the vendors that other people in your industry have endorsed.
- ⋏ Use it to meet the people you want to meet. LinkedIn allows you to search for people two degrees of separation away. That means anyone that knows someone who knows someone you know, can be contacted. This is an incredibly powerful way to get your foot in the door.
- ⋏ Link to content in your profile. If you have a blog or if you've written a quality article for a magazine, link to it. It helps build your credibility.

SEO your profile. Putting just a little bit of work into SEOing your profile could help your LinkedIn profile rank when someone types in your name. If you don't have a website setup under your name already, a LinkedIn profile can be a great way to build your reputation.

Google+ Pages

Google+ pages allows you to connect with Google+'s millions of users in a professional way. It helps you separate personal posts from business posts. Google+ also offers a number of unique features, such as the ability to segment who sees what on your page. Here's how to setup and use Google+ Pages.

Step 1: Getting Started

Start by going to http://www.google.com/+/business/ to get started.

Introducing Pages for Google+

A leap forward in building relationships between businesses and people

Create your Google+ Page

Step 2: Select a Category

Google has five different kinds of pages you can create. Each has a slightly different look and feel. Choose the one that best relates to the kind of page you want to create.

Step 3: Basic Information

Fill out some basic information about your page. Set the name of your page, your website and your privacy settings here.

Add your info

Product or Brand

Page name

Website (optional)

Select a category ▾

Your page will be publicly visible. Its content is appropriate for

Any Google+ user ▾ ⊙

☑ Yes, please keep me informed of future Pages releases and other relevant information.

☐ I agree to the Pages Terms and I am authorized to create this page.

CREATE

Step 4: Share Your Page

Once your page is up and running, Google+ will give you the opportunity to share it with the world. Just enter a brief message and it'll be posted to your wall.

Get the word out
Tell everyone about your new page

Tell your circles about this page...   Share on Google+

Note: this post will come from you, not from this page

Step 5: Posting on Your Page

Your page is now up and running. To begin adding content, just click "Post on Your Page."

Start the conversation

People want to hear from you! Start sharing photos, videos, links, and other interesting content publicly.

Post on your page

There are a few important things to know about posting.

First, if you want to post an image, a video or a web link, just click the corresponding button on the lower right corner. Any photos or videos you post will be added to the "Photos" or "Videos" tabs.

You can customize whether you want the post to be visible to everyone, or just a select group of people by canceling "Public" in the lower left and adding specific circles that you want to post to.

Stream

Public ×   + Add more people

Step 6: Get a Badge

Adding the ability for people to "+1" your page or land on your page from your website can be a big boon for your page. The best way to do this is through adding a badge. Just click "Get the badge" and add the HTML code to your website.

Connect your website

Grow your audience by making it easy for people to find and recommend your page. Place the Google+ badge or a small code snippet on your site.

Get the badge »

Step 7: Hangouts

One great way to connect with users is through hangouts. These are impromptu (or scheduled) video chat meetings. To use a hangout, just click the hangout button on the right.

Hangouts

Have fun with all your circles using your live webcam.

 Start a hangout

Tips for Connecting with Google+ Pages Users

- ⅄ Google+ Pages offers are few unique features that no other social networks offer. Taking advantage of these features will help you gain more readership, more followers and build more credibility.
- ⅄ Here are a few tips for using Google+ Pages.
- ⅄ Use your circles. Separate the different interest groups in your user base and post different messages to them. For example, you might post different messages to prospects, to customers, to suppliers and to the rest of the world.
- ⅄ Take advantage of the multimedia options. Google+ allows you to embed images and videos inside the post itself. This is an extremely rare feature that isn't available on Facebook or

Twitter. Furthermore, all the multimedia you post can be easily accessed in the Photos or Videos tabs.

- ⋏ Post long pieces of content when it makes sense. Unlike other social networks which cut off your content and require you to link you, Google+ Pages allows you to just post it all on your wall. This is great for event announcements, unique content and product promotions.

- ⋏ Actively promote your page to your Google+ friends and circles. While Google+ pages can be a powerful tool for communicating, people simply won't hear about it unless you talk about it often.

Assume your audience is sophisticated and tech savvy. Though Facebook has huge penetration, the majority of Google+ users are early adopters and people who like to test new technologies. As a result, by and large your followers will be very savvy. Don't give out basic content; instead use your Google+ Page to promote only the best of what you've got.

Pinterest

Pinterest is a relatively new social networking site with a twist. It's all about creating and sharing collections of images that you find around the web or create yourself. They call it themselves a "Virtual Pin Board' and their members use it to organize recipes, plan home improvement projects, share favorite books, plan weddings and more. You're only limited by your imagination.

Currently, to join Pinterest, you need to be invited. Without an account, you can browse and search what people a "pinning", but you can't enjoy any of the functionality.

Below is an example of what you might see by browsing the site without an account. However, if you sign up, you can follow specific people with interests common to yours. So if you're not interest in makeup or beading, you can choose to follow people with other interests.

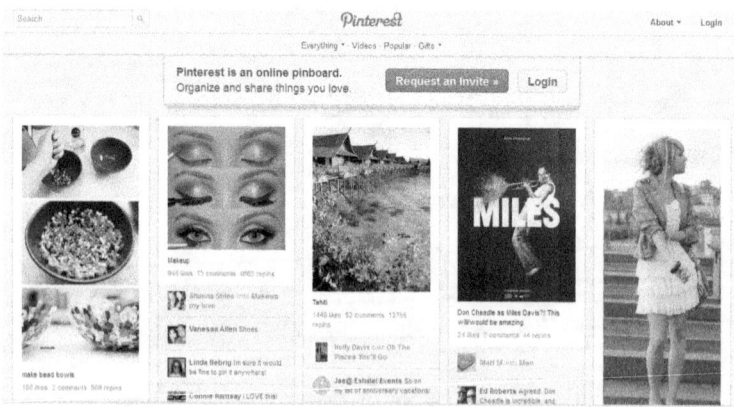

Pinterest currently has about 4 million users and about 80% of their audience is female, but there is definitely male representation on the site. With this large audience, it's relatively easy to secure an invitation and get started.

Here are two main ways you can get into Pinterest...

Method #1: Request an Invite from Pinterest

If you go to Pinterest.com, you can click the "Request an Invite" button.

On the next page, enter your email address and click "Request Invitation".

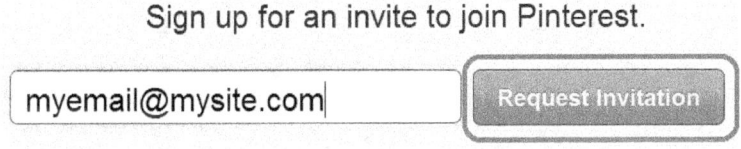

Once you've done that, you'll be greeted by this message.

Thanks! We'll send you an invite as soon as we can. In the meantime, **checkout some pins**.

How long it takes to get an invitation is unknown, so the best thing to do is actually try Method #2 and contact a member directly for an invite.

Method #2: Contact a Member Directly for an Invite

If you're active on other social media sites, chances are, you know somebody who is using Pinterest. Have a look on Facebook and if you see something like this, ask that person for an invitation.

Or if you look at someone's timeline, you might see a section dedicated to their Pinterest activity.

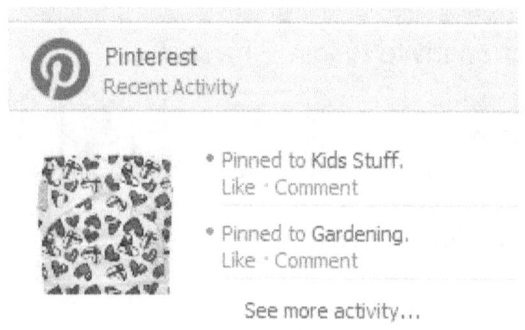

On Twitter, a Pinterest update looks something like this:

Faux stitching for your scrapbook.

pinterest.com/pin/2657124467...

11:43 AM - 4 Feb 12 via Pinterest | Embed this Tweet

← Reply   ⇄ Retweet   ★ Favorite

When you find someone using Pinterest, send them a message directly and ask if they don't mind sending you an invitation. All that person has to do is log into their account, fill out the "Invite Friends Form" and then you'll get the information via email. They can also choose to invite you by Facebook, so if that's the case, you'll get the invite through Facebook.

We'll demonstrate the email process in the next section.

Accepting Your Pinterest Invitation

After your friend sends the invite, you'll get an email that looks like this. The subject line will be "Check out my stuff on Pinterest":

Check out my stuff on Pinterest

Hi,

I set up a Pinterest profile where I can share the things I like and I want you to follow me so you can see it! Once you join Pinterest, you'll be able to create your own collections and share your taste.

Thanks,
Melissa

To sign up for Pinterest, follow the link below:

http://pinterest.com/invited/?email=▇▇▇▇▇▇&invite=▇▇▇▇

Click the link at the bottom of the email you received (we've blacked out the sensitive information in the link in our sample) and you can start creating your account.

Side note, if you're invited through Facebook, you'll see the invitation in your Notifications and it might look something like this:

But let's keep going through the process of accepting an email invite.

Setting Up Your Account

Once you click the link in the invitation email, you'll see a page that looks like this:

Congratulations! You've been invited to join Pinterest.

In order to use Pinterest, you have to either register with a Facebook or Twitter account. They say they do this because they believe it makes it easier for people to find you, cuts down on spam and you can easily share your updates with those sites. It doesn't matter if you start by registering with Facebook or Twitter, you can link both accounts at a later date.

We're going to go through the process by signing up with Twitter, so we click "Or sign up with Twitter."

Authorize Pinterest to use your account?

This application will be able to:

- Read Tweets from your timeline.
- See who you follow, and follow new people.
- Update your profile.
- Post Tweets for you.

Pinterest
By Cold Brew Labs
pinterest.com

A visual bookmarking utility.

← Cancel, and return to app

This application will **not be able to**:

- Access your direct messages.
- See your Twitter password.

Don't worry about Pinterest doing things with your Twitter account that you don't want it to. You have complete control and if you don't want Pinterest to update anything on Twitter, you can set it that way too. If it sounds good, click "Sign In" as shown above.

On the next page, you'll see that Pinterest automatically grabbed your avatar (we've blacked out this one for privacy reasons). Then you can choose a username, add your email address and password.

Click "Create Account" when you're done. Next you'll be presented with 28 categories that you can choose as being related to your interests. Pinterest uses this information to automatically follow people with common interests. You have to pick at least one category to continue.

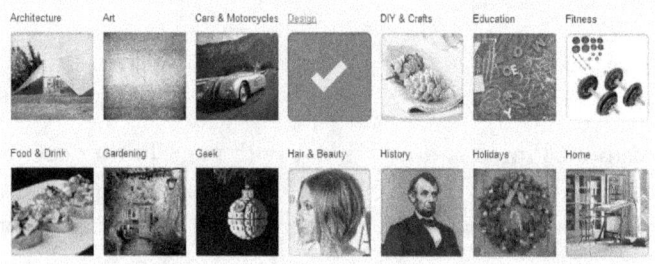

When you're done choosing, click "Follow People" at the bottom of the screen.

On the page page, you'll be able to see who you are now following and remove them, if you prefer. If everything's a-okay then you can start creating boards.

On the next page, you'll see five suggested boards you can create. You can edit these, delete these or do whatever you want. If you're not sure about all the boards you're going to create, you can just start with one and add as many as you want later. You can also see further suggestions to the right. If you click one of those, it will automatically be added to your list.

Create Your First Pinboards

Products I Love

Favorite Places & Spaces

Books Worth Reading

My Style

For the Home

Add

Create »

Pinboards are visual collections of things you love.

Other Pinboard Ideas:
+ Dream Home
+ Neighborhood Finds
+ Wedding Ideas
+ Favorite Recipes
+ Craft Ideas
+ Things for My Wall
+ Places I'd Like to Go
+ People I Admire
+ Party Ideas
+ Kid's Room

Click "Create" when you're done deciding on your boards. Again, you can add whatever you want or delete any boards later too. Now you're ready to get started with Pinterest!

RSS (Really Simple Syndication)

Following are four different platforms for using RSS. How can you not love a technology that spreads your message that you only have to set up once and it automatically works over and over and over.

Twitter Feed

If you regularly post your blog posts to Twitter and Facebook, why not have someone else do it for you instead? Twitter Feed will take your RSS feed, visit it every 30 minutes or so, find updates and automatically post them to Twitter and/or Facebook for you.

You can customize it to just post the title, the description or both. You can even include a thumbnail image on Facebook. It's easy to setup and maintain and can save you a lot of time if you blog regularly.

Here's how to setup Twitter Feed. Before you start, please have an RSS feed already setup, as well as a Twitter account and a Facebook account that you're logged into.

Step 1: Click Register

Go to http://www.twitterfeed.com. Click "Register" to begin the setup process.

Step 2: Complete the Registration Form

Fill out your email and password, then click "Create Account."

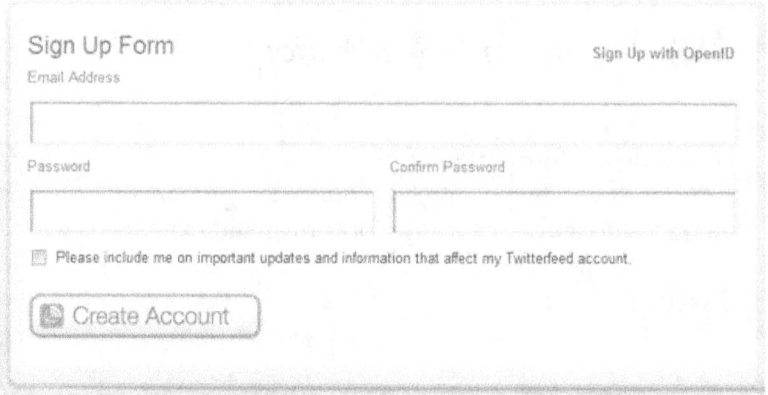

Step 3: Enter Your RSS Feed

You'll immediately begin the setup process. Enter your RSS feed into the topmost box.

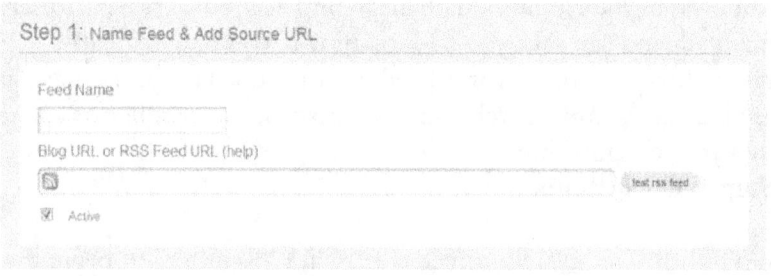

Step 4: Advanced Settings (Optional)

Click the "Advanced Settings" dropdown box to change the update frequency, sorting, level of detail to each post and so on. Click Step 2 when finished.

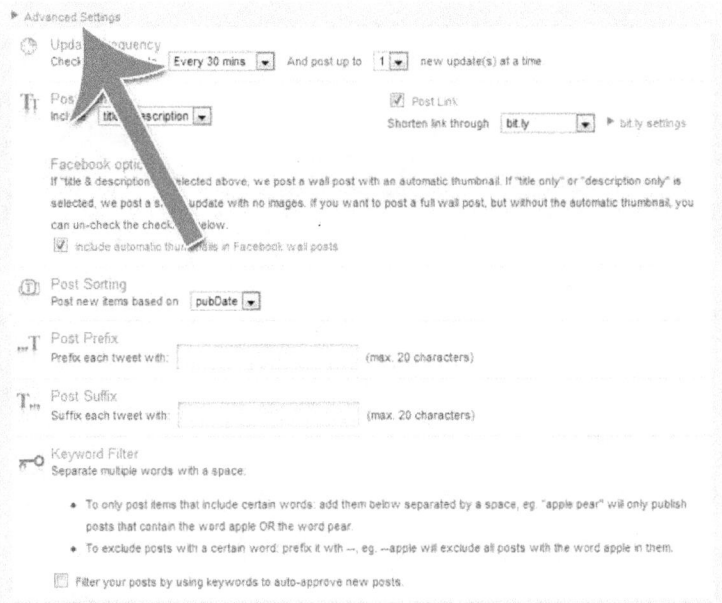

Step 5: Select Service, Twitter

Select whichever service you want to link to your RSS feed. Here we'll start with Twitter, then show Facebook.

Step 6: Authenticate Twitter

Click the "Authenticate Twitter" button to verify that you're the owner of the account.

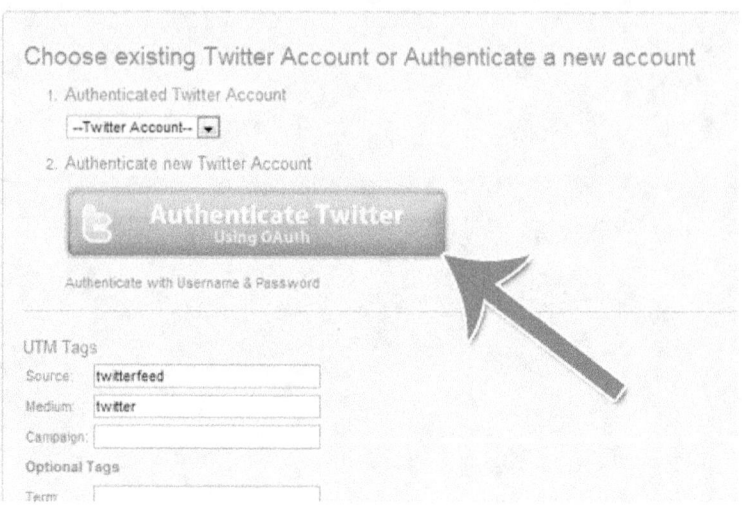

If you're already logged in, Twitter will prompt you with an authorization box.

Authorize twitterfeed to use your account?

This application will be able to:

- Read Tweets from your timeline.
- See who you follow, and follow new people.
- Update your profile
- Post Tweets on your behalf.

| Authorize app | No, thanks |

This application will not be able to:

- See your Twitter password.

Once authenticated, click "Create Service" to continue.

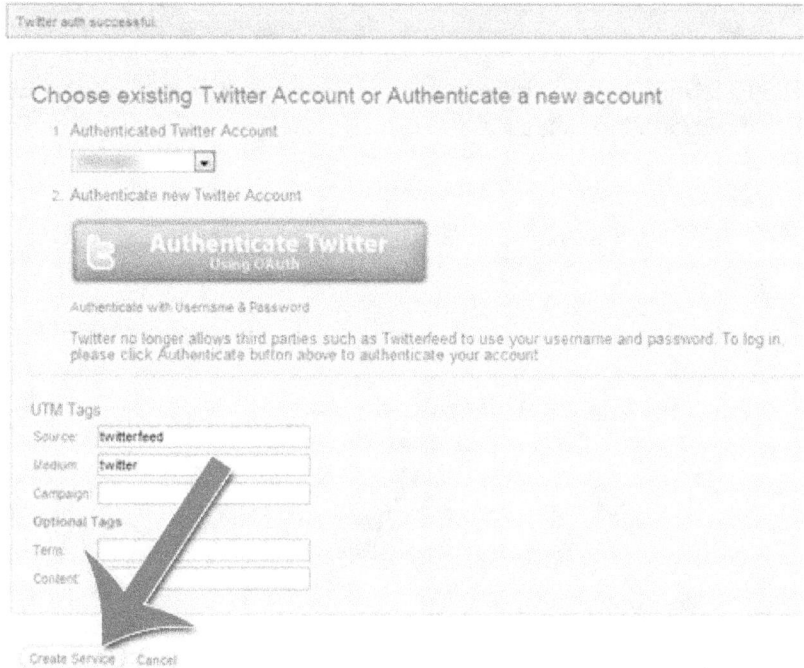

Step 7: Select Service, Facebook

If you just want to connect Twitter, then just click "All Done!" instead.
If you want to add Facebook as well however, click on Facebook to
repeat the process.

Step 8: Authenticate Facebook

Facebook will go through a similar process. Click "Connect with Facebook" to begin.

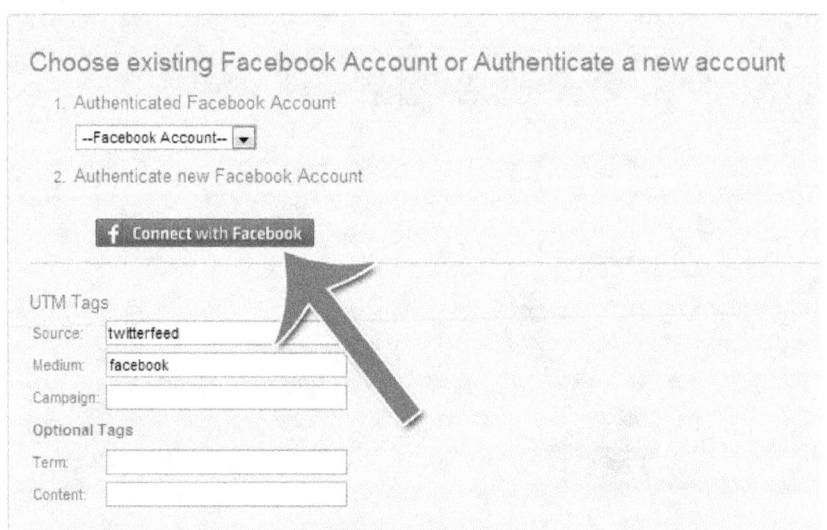

Click on "Allow" to grant TwitterFeed permission to post to your wall and pages.

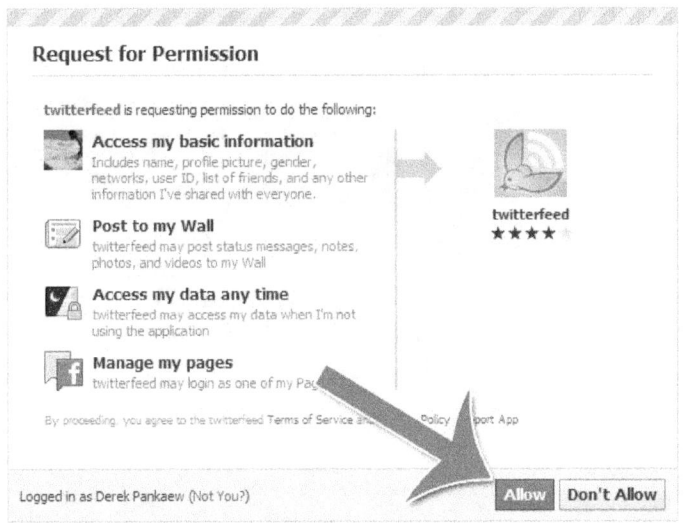

Finally, select which page or wall you want Facebook to post to, then click Create Service.

If you want to post to multiple Facebook pages, create another RSS link.

Step 9: Complete Setup

Click on "All Done!" on the services page once both Twitter and Facebook are setup.

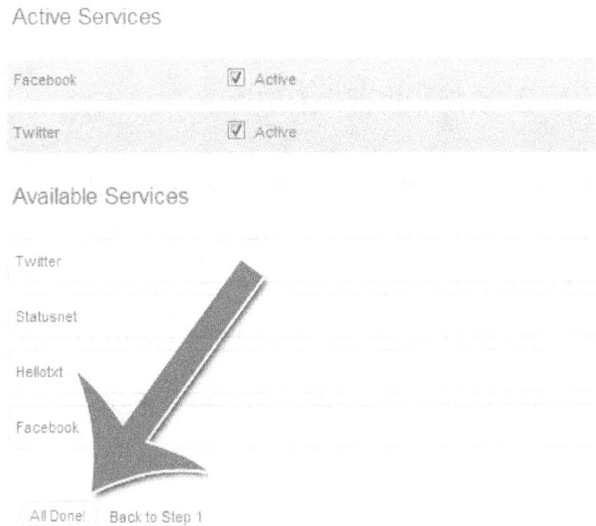

Finally, your setup completion page will be displayed.

Congratulations! Any time you post a blog post, within about 30 minutes Twitter Feed will read the post and post it on your Facebook page/wall as well as your Twitter feed. It's that easy!

Feedburner Publicize Tools

Feedburner has a ton of built-in tools designed to help blog owners share their feed better. Whether you want to ping other services when you post or allow other blog owners to share your feed, Feedburner makes it easy.

In this guide, we'll walk through all of FeedBurner's tools that allow you to publicize and share your feed more effectively. To start, you'll need to already have created a feed in Feedburner.

Accessing the Publicize Tools

To access the publicize tools, just click "Publicize" along the top navigation.

To navigate to the specific tool you want to use, just click one of the services under the Services navigation bar on the right.

Headline Animator
Display rotating headlines

BuzzBoost
Republish your feed as HTML

Email Subscriptions
Offer feed updates via email

PingShot
Notify services when you post

FeedCount
Show off your feed circulation

Socialize
Publish to the social web

Chicklet Chooser

Awareness API

Creative Commons

Password Protector

NoIndex

The Headline Animator

The headline animator will create an RSS feed box that'll automatically put the newest headlines in. You can place this box on a website for example and every time someone visits, they'll see the headline of your newest post.

Create a New Headline Animator

Clickthrough URL

http://feeds.feedburner.com/mixergy/oEWk

Theme

| 468x60 White ▼ | Revert to selected theme |

☑ Title

Amazingly Good Stuff

Width: 300   Font Size: 11 ▼   Color: #339900   ■■■■■□

Headlines

☐ **Wrap long headlines**   (not recommended for small Headline Animators)

Width: 300   Font Size: 13 ▼   Color: #000000   ■■■■■□

☑ Dates

Format: January 19, 2007 ▼

Width: 200   Font Size: 10 ▼   Color: #666666   ■■■■■□

Amazingly Good Stuff
Sample headline from feed
January 19, 2007   POWERED BY FEEDBURNER

Psst! You can **drag** title, date and headline to re-arrange on the canvas above!

Activate and save as: 468x60 White

Just set your options for how you want the box to look. A preview of how your box will look will appear towards the bottom. Click Activate to generate the code for the headline box.

BuzzBoost

Want to share more than just the headline of your post? BuzzBoost makes it easy. Just fill out your options, then click Activate. The JavaScript code can then be pasted onto any website to create a RSS feed box with anywhere between 1 to 15 posts.

Feed Settings

Number of items to display: 3

Open links in: New Window

Feed Content to Display

☑ Display feed title (or provide your own)

Amazingly Good Stuff

☐ Display favicon
   Woohoo! Favicon found at http://mixergy.com/favicon.ico

☐ Display item author name (if available)

☑ Display item content

   Plain Text   ITEM CONTENT FORMAT

   20 words   PLAIN TEXT EXCERPT LENGTH

☑ Display item publication date

   1/5/2007   DATE FORMAT

   Above Item Content   DATE LOCATION

☐ Show linked media from a podcast

☐ Display link to feed

Activate This service is **inactive**

Email Subscriptions

A lot of people would rather get their blog posts in their inbox, rather than having to visit your blog all the time or learn to use an RSS reader. That's easy, with email subscriptions. Just activate it, then once people are signed up they'll automatically get your blog posts by email.

Email Subscriptions

Give your biggest fans another way to keep up with your blog or podcast feed by placing an email subscription form on your site.

After you activate this service, FeedBurner will provide HTML code for a subscription form you should copy and place on your own site.

Note: Email Subscriptions requires that your FeedBurner account uses a valid email address. Visit My Account to double-check your settings.

FeedBurner Email Preview

View a sample message in HTML or Plain Text

How do I know which email format my subscribers will see?

Activate This service is **inactive**

Ping Shot

Instead of having other services refresh your feed, constantly taking up your bandwidth, you can just tell Feedburner to send those services a "ping" of data whenever you update your blog.
All you need to do is click Activate.

PingShot

Most web-based feed reading services will check for updates on their own time. Give 'em a push with PingShot.

√ Notify interested services when my feed changes

Activate This service is **inactive**

Feed Count

If you want to show off how many subscribers you have on your RSS feed, all you need to do is publish your Feed Count.

Select your button and text color and select whether you want a static or animated button. Then click Activate to generate the code.

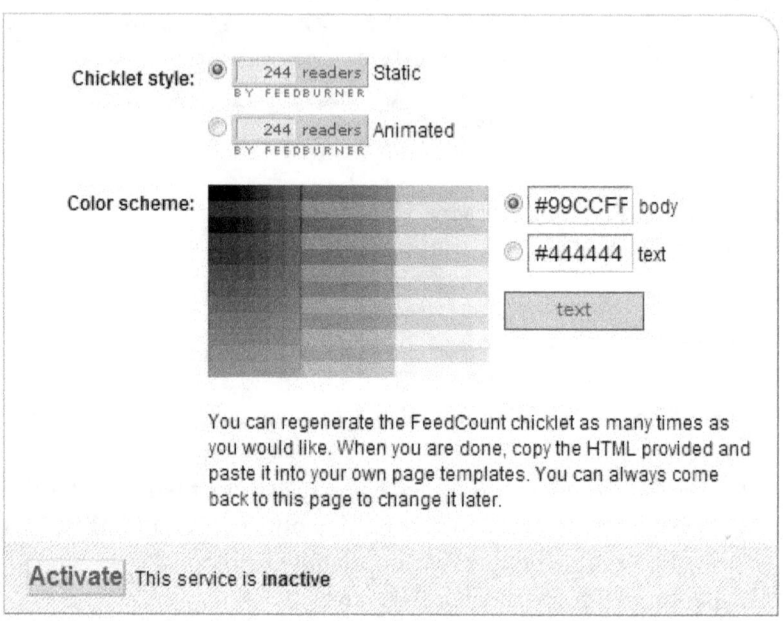

Socialize

Want to automatically post to your Facebook, Twitter or other social media accounts? Feedburner allows you to easily link other accounts to your feed.

Anytime you post on your blog, the post will also automatically be posted to the account(s) you specify.

To add more accounts to post to, just click "Manage Connections." Under formatting options, select how you want your posts to look, then click Activate to link the accounts.

Additional Tools

The tools we've just covered are the most important tools for publicizing your feed. In addition, there are also a few more tools and options you can change in the publicize options.

Chicklet Chooser

Awareness API

Creative Commons

Password Protector

NoIndex

Here's what each of these does:

Chicklet Chooser: Select a slightly different button to take people to your RSS feed.

Awareness API: Allow other developers to read your feed with software. This is useful if you want outside software to sort and use data from your blog.

Creative Commons: Choose the type of copyright your feed is protected under.

Password Protector: Require a password for people to read your feed. Note that this will deactivate the email subscription option.

NoIndex: Deny search engines access from your feed.

These are all the tools available to you in FeedBurner's publicize tools. As you can tell, it's easy to publish and use your RSS feed in many different ways, whether it's on your website, your Facebook page or even a friend's software.

FeedJournal

FeedJournal is a unique online service that allows you to turn one or more RSS feeds into a downloadable newspaper format PDF. In other words, it can turn any blog or combination of blogs into a newspaper. It's fast, easy to use and completely free as long as you're using just one feed. Combining multiple RSS feeds costs $59 a month. Here's how to turn your feed into a downloadable newspaper.

Step 1: Enter Your Email & RSS Feed

Go to http://www.feedjournal.com and scroll down. Under the heading "Generate your own free issue now!" enter your email address and RSS feed.

Generate your own free issue now!

Fill out the form below to generate a sample PDF using our basic service, free of charge.

E-Mail address

You will receive the link to the generated PDF newspaper by e-mail.

☑ FeedJournal may contact me

RSS or Atom feed

This must be a valid RSS or Atom feed with content owned by you.

Generate Your FREE Newspaper Now

Assuming FeedJournal is able to pull your RSS feed successfully, you'll see this message after a few seconds:

Your newspaper has been generated and a link to it has been sent to your email address. Please allow a few minutes for the e-mail to arrive in your inbox. We hope that you enjoy our services. Please contact us if you have any questions or comments.

Step 2: Open PDF in Email

Go to your email and find the message from FeedJournal. Click the link to open the PDF.

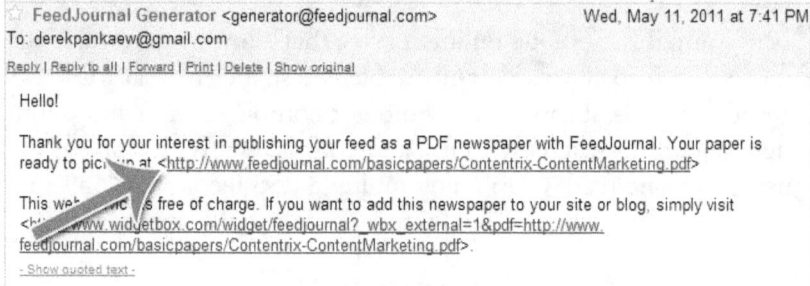

Step 3: View Online Newspaper

The PDF version of your RSS feed will open up. Here's a sample of what this looks like:

FeedJournal

FeedJournal Basic 5/1/2011 - 5/11/2011 feedjournal.com

7 Secrets to Avoid the A-List And Still Rake in Tons of Cash

Step 4: Multiple RSS Feed (Optional)

In order to aggregate multiple RSS feeds into one newspaper, you need to get the gold membership. Scroll down to the bottom to contact FeedJournal and sign up.

Gold Membership
Unlimited
Yes
Yes
Yes
Yes
Yes
Yes
Yes
Yes
Yes
Yes
Yes
Yes
Yes (with custom size)
$59/month
Contact Us for a free Demo!

It's that easy! Turning your RSS feed into an online newspaper can take as little as 5 minutes with the help of FeedJournal.

WP-o-Matic

WP-o-Matic is a powerful source of condensing multiple sources of RSS feeds into one website.

Let's say you run a radio show and want to condense the blogs of all your show hosts. Or you run a company and want to condense all your employee's blogs into a company blog. Or you personally run a podcast, a website, a newsletter, etc and want to condense them all into one blog.

Instead of having to go into all these sources individually to copy and paste the posts, WP-o-Matic will allow you to easily download all their RSS feeds in one place and automatically post the resulting feed.

Here's how to setup and use WP-o-Matic.

Step 1: Download and Install WP-o-Matic plugin

Go to your plugins tab and do a search for WP-o-Matic. Click Install to install the plugin.

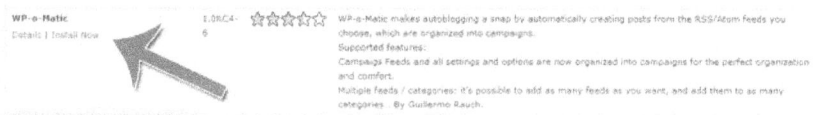

Step 2: Go to WP-o-Matic's Settings

To begin the setup process, go to your Settings tab and go to WP-o-Matic's settings.

Step 3: Run the Simplepie Test

The first thing you need to do when you install WP-o-Matic is install Simplepie. Basically this makes sure your server will work with WP-o-Matic. Most major servers will pass the test.

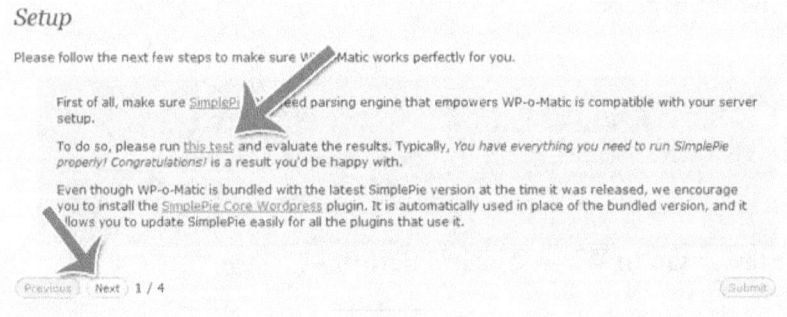

Click next after completing the test. It should just take 30 seconds.

Step 4: Check Your Time Settings

Make sure your time settings are correctly set. WP-o-Matic needs to time its updates, so getting your time settings right is essential.

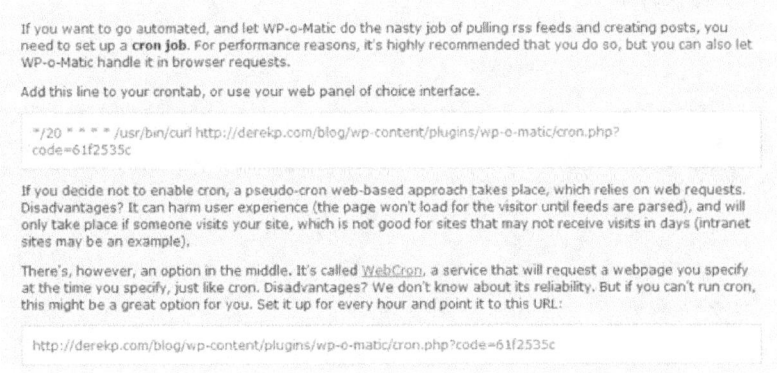

Setup

Please follow the next few steps to make sure WP-o-Matic works perfectly for you.

Timing is a key aspect of this type of feed aggregating software.

For WP-o-Matic to work properly, you have to make sure server time is accurate, and that the correct timezone is configured here (hint: **Date and Time** subsection)

Make sure the following settings are correct:

UTC time: 10 May, 2011 11:14:52
Your time: 10 May, 2011 11:14:52

Do not proceed unless time is configured properly.

Previous   Next   2 / 4   Submit

Step 5: Install Cron Job

This is the trickiest part of the installation. In order for WP-o-Matic to work, you need to install what's called a "cron job," which is basically a recurring command given the server. This has to be installed onto the server, not in Wordpress.

When you get to Step 3 of the setup process, you'll see a line of code like this:

If you want to go automated, and let WP-o-Matic do the nasty job of pulling rss feeds and creating posts, you need to set up a **cron job**. For performance reasons, it's highly recommended that you do so, but you can also let WP-o-Matic handle it in browser requests.

Add this line to your crontab, or use your web panel of choice interface.

```
*/20 * * * * /usr/bin/curl http://derekp.com/blog/wp-content/plugins/wp-o-matic/cron.php?
code=61f2535c
```

If you decide not to enable cron, a pseudo-cron web-based approach takes place, which relies on web requests. Disadvantages? It can harm user experience (the page won't load for the visitor until feeds are parsed), and will only take place if someone visits your site, which is not good for sites that may not receive visits in days (intranet sites may be an example).

There's, however, an option in the middle. It's called WebCron, a service that will request a webpage you specify at the time you specify, just like cron. Disadvantages? We don't know about its reliability. But if you can't run cron, this might be a great option for you. Set it up for every hour and point it to this URL:

```
http://derekp.com/blog/wp-content/plugins/wp-o-matic/cron.php?code=61f2535c
```

Each server will have a different way to setup a cron job. Here we'll just show how it's done in Hostgator. Most other hosts will have a similar installation process.

First log into your web host and go to the cPanel. Then find the cron job tab. If you can't find it, press CTRL+F and type in "cron".

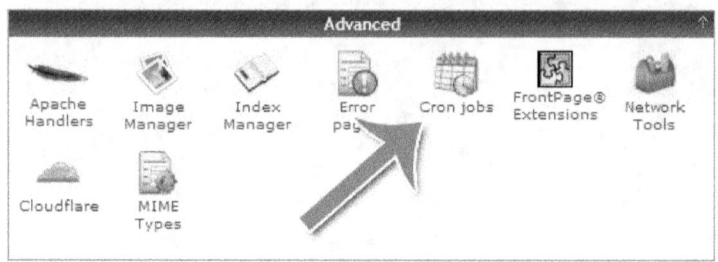

Next, you'll *either* paste in the whole code, including the numbers and asterisks, or you'll have to translate them into their respective time fields.

The */20 * * * * part of the code is the *time* part of the code. The rest is the Unix code that's to be executed at the time specified by the first part of the code.

In hostgator, you'll need to specify that the command is to be executed every 20 minutes, then paste in the code in the "command" box.

Add New Cron Job

* Crons with intervals less than once per 15 minutes will be automatically adjusted per TOS.

Common Settings:	-- Common Settings --	
Minute:	*/20	-- Common Settings --
Hour:	*	Every hour (*)
Day:	*	Every day (*)
Month:	*	Every month (*)
Weekday:	*	Every weekday (*)
Command:	content/plugins/wp-o-matic/cron.php?code=61f2535c	

Add New Cron Job

Again, in other servers you might just copy and paste the whole code. In hostgator, you need to break up the time part of the code, then paste the rest into the command box.

This is the trickiest part of the installation. If you have difficulty, just email your webhost and a tech support admin will likely be able to assist you.

After the cron job is installed, your WP-o-Matic plugin setup is complete. Next you'll need to setup your RSS feeds.

Step 6: Add a Campaign

It's time to setup your first campaign. Click on "Add Campaign" on the left hand side of the WP-o-Matic settings.

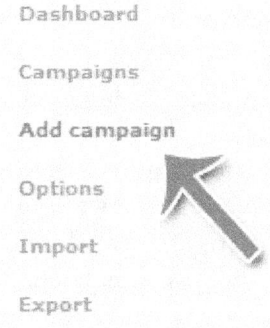

Dashboard

Campaigns

Add campaign

Options

Import

Export

Step 7: Basic Setup

Give your campaign a name. The name's only visible to you. Check the box to make sure the campaign is active and give your campaign an ID if you want.

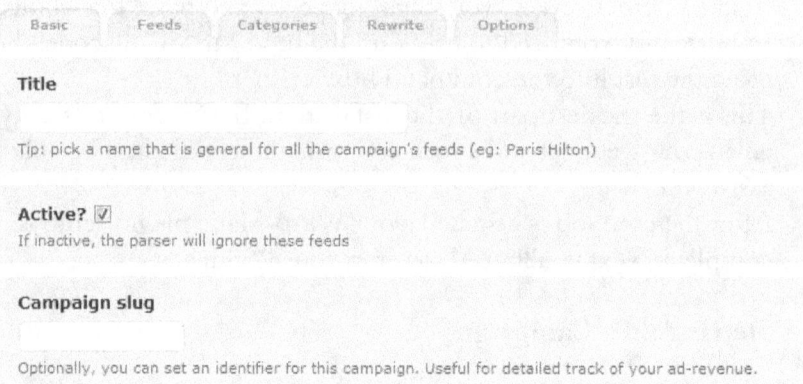

Title

Tip: pick a name that is general for all the campaign's feeds (eg: Paris Hilton)

Active? ✓
If inactive, the parser will ignore these feeds

Campaign slug

Optionally, you can set an identifier for this campaign. Useful for detailed track of your ad-revenue.

Step 8: Enter Your Feeds

Navigate to the Feeds tab. Enter up to four feeds. Any time a new post appears on one of these feeds, it'll then automatically be posted to your blog.

In general, it's best to just have one feed per campaign. That way, you can disable the whole campaign without interfering with the rest.

The exception is if feeds are very close in nature. Say you're running a company blog with three people: Jared, Kacey and Max. If Kacey and Max only have 1 blog each, you'll put them into separate campaigns. But if Jared had two, you might just put both of Jared's blogs into the same campaign.

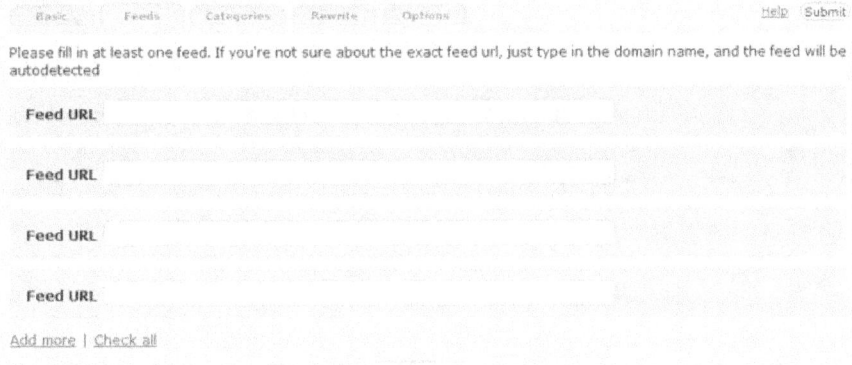

Step 9: Categories & Rewrites

In the Categories tab, select one of the categories to put the posts under.

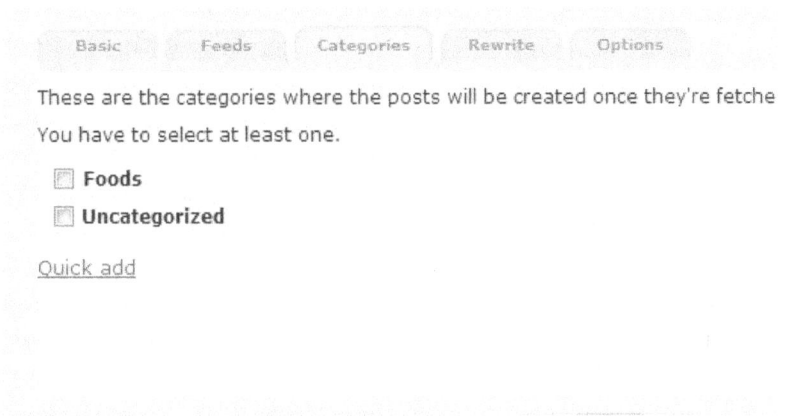

The rewrites tab is strictly optional. It allows you to substitute words imported from the feed for other words.

For example, if you wanted to substitute all swear words for less offensive words, you could. Most people would just leave this tab blank.

Basic   Feeds   Categories   Rewrite   Options

Want to transform a word into another? Or link a specific word to some webs

Origin

☐ **RegEx**

☐ **Rewrite to:**

☐ **Relink to:**

Add more

WP-o-Matic 1.0RC4-6 — Copyright ©2008 Guille

Step 10: Options

The options tab allows you to customize a lot of how WP-o-Matic behaves. Each of these options comes with an explanation underneath.

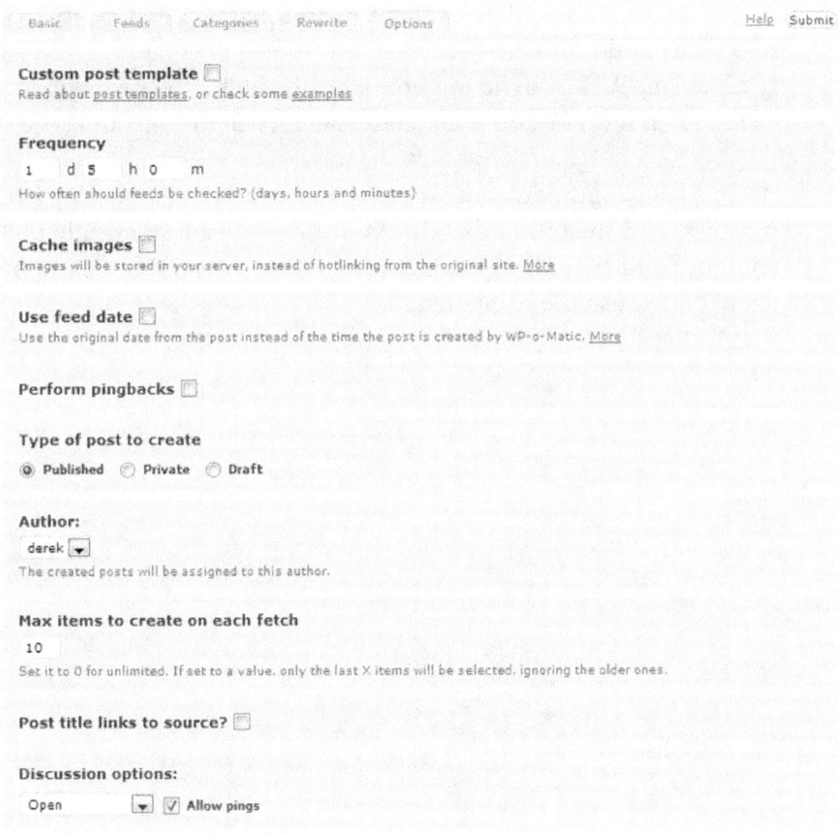

Basic
Feeds
Categories
Rewrite
Options
Help
Submit
Custom post template
Read about post templates, or check some examples
Frequency
1 d 5 h 0 m
How often should feeds be checked? (days, hours and minutes)
Cache images
Images will be stored in your server, instead of hotlinking from the original site. More
Use feed date
Use the original date from the post instead of the time the post is created by WP-o-Matic. More
Perform pingbacks
Type of post to create
Published
Private
Draft
Author:
derek
The created posts will be assigned to this author.
Max items to create on each fetch
10
Set it to 0 for unlimited. If set to a value, only the last X items will be selected, ignoring the older ones.
Post title links to source?
Discussion options:
Open
Allow pings

Step 11: Submit & Fetch

Click the submit button in the upper right to finish your campaign setup. Assuming everything was setup properly, you'll see a completed setup box like this:

Campaign added successfully. Edit it or fetch it now
Basic
Feeds
Categories
Rewrite
Submit

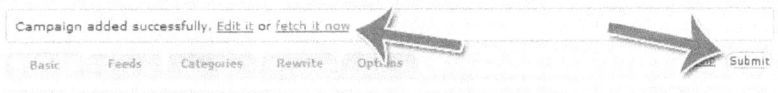

At this point, WP-o-Matic will automatically fetch new posts from the RSS feeds and populate your blog with those posts.
If you want WP-o-Matic to automatically fetch blog posts now, just click "fetch it now" and it'll collect the last 15 posts from those feeds.

All this setup shouldn't take more than 60 minutes, assuming no troubles with the cron job. Now your blog will automatically pull new content from these RSS feeds, with little to no work from you until you choose to pause the campaign.

Article Marketing is Dead

For those new to internet marketing, for many years Article Marketing has been a key to getting your website to raise in rankings on the search engines. The act of writing content (information) and posting it on different article directories had a twofold bonus.

First by posting articles on many different directories it gives you the opportunity to spread the word to a huge audience. Prospects will search the directories for you key word, find your article, become intrigued with what you had to say and click a link through to your site.

The methodology goes that upon arriving on your site, the prospect will be pre-sold on your expertise and be more likely to trust and buy from you.

Secondly article marketing was used by internet marketers to inflate their popularity. As we have mentioned else where the more links you have pointing to your site are considered votes by the search engines and thus elevate your position in the search engine rankings when people searched for your keyword. Go here for a more extensive explanation of back linking by Google itself.
http://tradeshowroi.org/influence-videos/

Thus Internet Marketers found the more articles you had pointing to your site the better. Yet who had time to write hundreds if not thousands of articles. So software was developed to spin articles --a term which means using some type of software to create similar versions of the same article. Basically the software takes a word and replaces it with something similar. An example may be
"John walked down the road." The word 'walked' is then replaced with 'strolled.' So you now have:"John strolled down the road."

Simple enough, right? As you can see, with an article of 500 words and say 100 of them are replaceable how many variations you can come up with. The problem became that when the software was not sophisticated it resulted in garbage sounding content. Taking the same sentence as before, replace 'walked' with 'hop' and 'road' with 'expressway.' Now you have you have the sentence: "John hopped down the expressway," which is not quite the same as the original and far from compelling.

The point being, the internet quickly became inundated with worthless articles who's only purpose was to get links back to a website. Well Google finally got fed up and in 2011 changed their algorithms to devalue all the links from the articles and article directories. This was part of their Panda Update, and with it came the death of article marketing.

Well, not really. The original reason for doing articles is still valid even if the links back to the author's sites do not count as much. Putting out well written highly educational content is the basis of this book. Present yourself as an expert and gain trust in the process. Rinse and repeat.

Mobile Websites

The mobile phone use statistics are staggering. The idea that more people will access the web by their phone than by a pc is mind boggling. Not having a mobile website is not an option, what is an option is what you offer via a mobile site.

Depending on your Industry this may vary greatly. Prospects require different information from their mobile device than from a personal computer. It is imperative to find out what your prospects are looking for when they do a mobile search. I know this sounds like common sense, but is rarely acted upon.

If all your prospect needs from you is contact information, then putting your complete catalog online will only make it more cumbersome and possibly slower. If you don't want your prospects calling the corporate office, then don't put a tap to call button on every web page. Are coupons important or not important to your mobile viewers? These are all points to consider when creating your mobile site that must be asked and answered before creating your site.

There is also speculation Google gives preference to websites with a mobile version in the search-Engine rankings.

Having a dedicated subdomain, such as m.mycompany.com instead of yoursite.mobi for mobile is an on going debate. It appears the big players are going with m.mycompany. The best advice I have heard is to create the m.mycompany and buy the mycomapny.mobi and just sit on it in case that turns out to be the best selection. Either way a simple re-direct script installed on your main domain can forward you mobile viewers to the proper URL or web address. The newer mobile softwares also detect what type of mobile device you are using and optimize the site to the mobile device. Meaning most sites look fine on almost any device.

Tips for Mobile Websites

- Quick to load
- Easy to navigate with fat fingers
- Tap to Call (if appropriate)
- Interactive Map with directions (if appropriate)
- Simple clear images
- All information should only be 2 to 3 taps away
- Easy to read (no small type)
- Have what your prospects need (Not what makes your company look good)
- Lead capture form (or forward to web page with capture form)
- Opportunity to opt in to SMS campaign
- Coupon (if appropriate)
- Some type of interactive application (Poll, quiz, games)
- Links to social sites

Follow up Campaign

We made it, it is finally time to collect a lead and turn the lead into a sale. I think we have all heard the stats before, they change from study to study but they all say the same thing, it takes repeated contacts to make a sale.

The Sales & Marketing Club of Los Angeles conducted a study that showed that 81% of sales closed on the 5th sales call, while only 10% closed on the 4th sales call.

The Dartnell Corporation did a study that concluded that only 10% of all salespeople will actually make 5 attempts to close a sale.

CEIR (Center for Exhibition Industry Research) says that studies show that 80% of exhibitors do not follow up on their leads from trade shows.

According to University of Massachusetts Center for Marketing Communications, 43% of prospective buyers receive material they have requested after they have already made a buying decision. Another 18 never receive the information at all.

So why do so few salespeople follow through and make the extra calls? If it only happened to a few people who did not make the contacts I would say they were lazy, untrained, or didn't care. But since it happens to almost everyone I would say - who knows, who cares.

The fact of the matter is without a predetermined, structured program, it does not happen and even with a plan it rarely happens. Whether you use Trade Show ROI or some other company, the only way to make sure follow up emails or calls happens is to hire an outside vender, or create your own follow up department.

Considering the massive amount of work creating a massive web presence takes let's look at two possible situations.

Example 1: Generic

You have done nothing this book has suggested so far, and are only interested in generating leads and sales through follow up campaigns.

Doing the follow up campaign alone will probably put you miles ahead of all your other competitors. The follow system will build rapport, give the prospect a chance to get to know you, present your product and over time hopefully make a sale to a certain percentage of your prospects.

Example 2: Expert

You have spent the last two months laying the ground work to create your company as the "go-to" Expert in your Industry. Your content is not only fun and interactive, it is highly educational. Everywhere prospects look, they find your company with third-party social proof reinforcing your Industry Expert Status. Your competition is not on the same playing field as you. You own the conversation and your new prospect wants to be connected with you.

Now, let's take a look at lead generation to follow up cycle:

You are a company showing at a trade show event. The goal is to build contacts, leads and relationships with potential prospects. Then use that information to to follow up campaigns.

Day of booth visit

You collect the lead at the show.

Along with about 150 other vendors, you send a text that night thanking the prospect for visiting your booth. No difference between generic and expert example.

Night of end of the Show

You send an email again thanking them for visiting your booth and explaining how and when your prize drawing will be. This email will have fewer competitors (maybe 20) as most will not email the prospect until the leads have been passed off back at the office. Still, no difference between expert and generic example.

Campaign Day Three

Prospect receives' voice mail broadcast

Prospect try's to remember which booth this company was, and is becoming familiar with the name, Prospect is being bombard with emails and texts from other companies. Still, no difference between generic and expert.

Day Five.

You send a poll via text. (Qualification begins)

Prospect decides it is time to do a little research. She searches the generic company, finds a website, Facebook page and twitter account. Thinks this is someone to keep in mind.

She now searches the expert company and is blown away by two pages of search results, including links to your website, blog, YouTube videos, SlideShare, Pinterest on and on. She clicks on her favorite and is pleased to find it is not boring company info, but some great engaging information that will be perfect for her next presentation.

She is actually enjoying doing the research and is thinking she is really going to look good to her manger with all this useful information, when she explains what she learned at the trade show. Now there is no comparison between the generic company and the Industry Expert.

Day Six and beyond.

The generic company will have a chance with repeated follow up and over time build a bond, since by now most if not all the other competitors have stopped following up on the majority of their leads.

*The Expert company is now in an incredible position. Not only does the prospect open the communications being sent, they look forward to the marketing messages, they are becoming raving fans. They start talking about you to their fellow workers and even their friends. Life is good when you are the top dog in your Industry. **It has become fun to grow your business again.***

The Follow Up from the Beginning

The idea behind the follow up system is to start with a qualification process, dividing the prospects into three categories.

Category 1 are un-responsive leads and are moved to a long term electronic (sms-email) drip feed. The cost is minimal and a long term drip feed will keep your Company Name top of mind. Should their needs change in the future you will be in great shape to re-enter them into the normal follow up system.

Category 2 leads are responsive but not ready to buy. They receive the full 26 week follow up system with expectations of turning these leads into sales by wowing them with educational fun and interactive communications. You get them to like and trust your company as you are now the Industry Expert.

Category 3 leads are the 3% to 5% who are ready to buy. They are put into an accelerated four week follow up program designed to be implemented in conjunction with the salesperson.

The following are different forms of follow up techniques which are sprinkled throughout the sequence. Your prospects will all react differently to different forms of media. The key here being to use as many different types of messages as possible to make sure we hit the proper hot spot of each prospect, also allowing for the different types of media prospect's use to receive the message.

The first step in any follow up sequence is acquiring the lead, so of to the trade show we go.

Lead Acquisition

The first draft started this section with "Using today's technology acquiring leads is simple." After attending a food trade show recently, I realize the use of that quote is wrong. Each booth had a Point of Sale terminal and each attendee was given an ID card as they entered the show.

The software was designed to take orders at the show and includes a module for acquiring information requests from the prospects. The lead is then forwarded to the sales person. This, all in all a pretty impressive system, at least in theory.

The show hosted a couple hundred vendors and I will guess 10,000 plus attendees and lasted from 10 AM to 5 PM. Needless to say I was more interested in how the vendors interacted with the prospects and how leads were being collected.

I did see one set of sheets at a booth titled Lead Contact Info with all the appropriate columns. It was about ¾ of the way through the show when I saw it and it was unused. I guess this makes sense because of the availability of the high tech equipment.

I don't have exact facts as I was only attending the show and I was only able to see a small portion of the booths at one time. Yet I did not see or hear one vendor ask a person to enter a request for information (giving the vendor a reason to contact them for follow up). When I asked a vendor to contact me, they fumbled through the system, taking several minutes to accomplish the task.

As I walked past booth after booth of vendors talking to themselves, standing with arms crossed or even casually talking to prospects I wanted to grab them by the collar and yell "Look at all the money walking by." Not to say there were not dozens and dozens of booths with lines taking orders, which are awesome, but once this happens there is no ability to acquire lead information from the people walking by who didn't want to wait in line and maybe said they would come back but never did.

Yes there are lots of ways to acquire leads these days at trade shows, and they include:

- Badge Readers

- Buying complete attendee list

- Fishbowl

- Kiosk

- POS Terminal

- Lead form

- SMS (Text messaging)

Each has their own pros and cons

- Ease of use for prospect

- Ease of use for company collecting

- Degree of qualification

- Ease of entering information

- Ease if using information

- Amount of Information collected

I am sure there are many more options, yet unless you enter the show with a well lay-ed out strategy for acquiring the leads, whether the booth is slow or busy and train the salespeople to implement the plan, no system will work. One advantage in today's technology is to the practice of collecting as many leads as possible, qualified or not as opposed to only collecting highly qualified leads. Let's look at both scenarios:

In the qualified lead scenario, once you have gone through the few leads you acquired, you are done and the benefits of the show are pretty much ended. Yes, you have some brand recognition but in the current personalized, social marketing atmosphere, brand advertising has less and less effect. It does not matter how good your follow up system is, once you are out of leads to enter into the system, game over.

Also if you are counting on your salespeople to close the sale with these qualified leads you may be sadly disappointed, if your competition has decided to become the Industry Expert and have other plans for your highly qualified leads.

In the collect-all-the-leads-you-can scenario, you can quickly and very inexpensively qualify the leads electronically and have dozens, if not hundreds of leads to follow.. Maybe even more importantly, with technology, human error is removed. Just because the prospect does not seem overly excited about your product, is not feeling well, or any number of other reasons that doesn't mean they are not a great lead. Let the prospect decide for themselves by engaging in your follow up system.

Was I wrong with my original draft saying acquiring the leads is the easy part? Yes and no. It is simple as long as you are prepared, know what you want to accomplish, know how you are going to accomplish it, train your salespeople how to accomplish it and finally and most important, implement your plan.

Direct Response Marketing.

Ok you now have the lead but why Direct Response Marketing.

- ▲ Each message contains a call to action- compelling prospect to take action now.

- ▲ Is designed to promote your benefits and USP to make you the obvious choice.

- ▲ Creates total differentiation between you and your competitors

- ▲ Ability to get instant response

- ▲ Easy to Track

- ▲ Answers the unspoken question on every prospect's mind:

"Why should I do business with you vs. each and every competitive option available to   me, including doing nothing?"

According to Chet Homes author of *The Ultimate Sales Machine* at any one time

3% Buying Now ($$$$)
6 -7 % Open To Buying ($$$)
30% Not thinking about Buying ($$)
30% Don't think they are interested ($)
30% Know they are not interested

The goal by combining direct response marketing and the 26-week follow up system is to not only turn the 3% into buyers, but move the 6 to 7% that are open to making a purchase into a sale. This is where most programs are done, yet with the follow up system you aggressively, yet gently push the 30% *not thinking about buying* into the *open to buying* bracket. While at the same time drip feeding the *Don't think they are interested* bracket so you will top of the mind should they move up the ladder. The *know they are not interested* will opt out of the system, self-cleaning the list for you.

The frame work for the messages is based on being:

- Immediate
- Personalized
- Continuous
- Qualify and Segment
- Multi-media
- Engaging
- Have Purpose

SMS (Text Messaging)

In conjunction with a QR code, SMS will rapidly be everywhere you look, shortly followed by a huge decline in use. In general, I've found that most marketers believe QR codes to be ineffective. If not used properly SMS is not only a waste of money it can alienate your prospects.

Picture yourself walking through a trade show and half the booths have a sign saying text "show" to 23456 to win a trip to Hawaii. Maybe when you first get to the show you are focused on what you are looking for. Yet once the show wears on and you are moving slower why not enter, Hawaii sounds good, you can always opt out later after the drawing.

Better yet, why not opt-in to win that 128" HD TV being promoted at the booth across the isle? And while you are at it, why not send a text to the rest of your company employee's back at the office and have them opt in too? Come to think of it, that TV would go great in the break room.

I guess I got a little off track here. Point is, SMS is not sounding so good now right? If you start with the mindset that SMS is going to get you tons of qualified leads, right off the bat you might think it is a waste. If you have the mindset all these non-prospects are taking advantage of you, you may again think it is a waste.

The reality is that people who opt-in to an SMS campaign or giveaway are, for a brief moment, giving their contact information – a way to further upsell to them. But you must realize that once the drawing is over for that exclusive Hawaii trip or 128" HD TV, a vast majority of the people will opt out the moment you send them a text. This is twofold – it eliminates the unqualified, uninterested prospects, but it also confirms qualified ones. If you communicate in a way as not to appear too spammy, you might actually make sales out of SMS targeting and be smiling to the bank. Compare that to a company that ends up with a huge list of unqualified uninterested opt-ins and sends a nasty text telling the people the drawing was meant for prospect and to opt out if you are not a prospect. Sounds absurd but it happens. Cool for you, since most of the prospects will opt out also.

The best way to qualify prospects with SMS is polls, request for more information, surveys and just plain asking. Since the prospect is likely receiving many texts, the content is of extreme importance. If the texts are just sales requests and un wanted information, the prospects will quickly opt out. It is not like email where they can be ignored. Open rate for SMS is estimated at over 95% and usually within five minutes, if you are wasting your prospects time you will be quickly removed.

If you are delivering helpful, fun, interesting messages your prospect will look forward to your text and be more likely to respond back. A campaign of just SMS will be very difficult to be effective, unless coupons are part of your process. Combining the SMS messages with a dozen other message types is very effective.

For those of my generation, a QR code is just an image that can be scanned by a smart phone. You download a QR code reader app and then basically just take a picture of the code. Embedded in the image is a code that can send your phone to a web site, bring up a phone number to text into a campaign or even bring up a form to be filled out. It's most popular use is to take the phone to a coupon which can be stored on the phone or on a web site.

Text TradeShow

71441

Email

Which would you prefer: the typical email telling you how great their company is and pushing you to grab the latest, newest widget on sale for the next 187 seconds? Or the following image of an email?

"Here, try this."

Dear <First>,

I have no idea why I haven't heard from you yet, but like the fellow in the doorway in the cartoon above, I'm doing my best to offer you a simple solution that will change your results in business, for good.

I can offer it, but I can't take the swing for you.

PLEASE CALL ME

So what am I asking you to do? Simply click the button above so we can set up a time to meet. That's it. Simple enough, but guaranteed to make a difference in your business. Won't you start that process by clicking the button now?

Sincerely,

Email Keys

- Make sure the from name is recognizable. Meaning Green Barbells compared to Sales
- The Subject line is as important as any Display ad headline
- Offer useful Information not all sales
- Include a call to action even if it just goes to an interesting article or video
- Be consistent. Once every few months will get spammed or opted out
- Use a major email provider to increase deliverability. Saving money here is a mistake
- Test deliver email format to make sure emails look good
- Keep emails short
- Always use a P.S.
- Track opens

Snail Mail

Envelopes – Postcards – Lumpy mail

Good housekeeping did a survey to find out what's the first thing people do when they get home from work. They found that the first thing they do is open their mail! And guess what? They open it over their trash can!

You, me, and everyone else, opens their mail the same way. They put their mail into piles...at least in their mind.

Contrary to belief, snail mail is making a comeback. Learning to pass the all-important A pile-B pile decision is still the difference between an effective campaign and throwing money in the trash.

Being an established Industry expert is going to greatly enhance your mail open rate. Once your prospect becomes a fan and is interested in what funky message you will send next they will look for your name and open anything. Still there is no sense in taking chances so extreme care must be used with each mailing.

In the early stages of the campaign, hand addressed envelopes with no return address will receive the highest open rates of sealed envelopes. Oversized color postcards will be read the most, since no effort is needed to open; they stand out and don't fit well into the mail stack. Yet both of these will often be stopped at the gate keeper's desk and never make it to the decision maker. The real attention getter and wow factor is with lumpy mail.

A package just calls out for attention. The package or oversized stuffed envelope is almost always put on top of the mail stack since nothing will stay neatly on top of it. I recently received a bank bag in the mail, while with my daughter. She asked what it was and I explained it was a marketing piece and just had some sales information in it. We were not even half way up the drive way and she was opening it. Even knowing there was nothing good in it and nothing for her, she just had to open it and see what was inside.

One of my mentors used to send basketballs in a package with a note stating the ball is now in your court. Can you image how many people the prospect told about that. Sure lumpy mail is expensive, but if you think of the cost compared to the result it is actually pretty inexpensive. The key is to be specific as to who you address it to. It can be a major waste of money if you have not already per-qualified the prospect. It does not matter how much you wow someone if they don't want your product they still will not want your product.

The key to any successful mail campaign is repeated contacts. One letter, postcard, lumpy mail will have little, if any, result. When combined with repeated contacts, different forms of media, mail can be highly personalized and very profitable.

Voice Broadcasts

This is a rather new technology and the verdict is still out. You are able to send a voice message that goes directly to a mobile phones voice mail. The idea is, it will not be perceived as a tele-marketing message, but as an individually sent call that you missed and went into voice mail.

At first it seems great, the night of day the prospect visited your booth you could send a voice broadcast thanking them for stopping by and reminding them of when your drawing will be. Thus helping prospects remember your booth while it might still be fresh in their minds.

The message would seem personal, timely and probably be saved for future listening. It would also stand out as almost every other competitor will be doing it via text messaging.

Now the reality. Almost everyone is checking their phones for messages, especially if they are out of town. If it only happens a few times, they will think they just missed the call somehow. Yet if it happens to often they will quickly catch on. Worse many people use their phones as wake up alarms so the phone is near their head at night. If you were to send a message in the middle of the night, the phone may beep, wake the person up thinking there was an emergency only to find out it was a mass sales call, probably losing that customer for good.

Voice broadcasts can be very effective but must be used with discretion and a well thought out strategy.

Webinars

Webinars are the key to the kingdom. One of the fastest and most effective forms of promoting a company and or selling a product is a webinar. Typical webinars are power point presentations while one or more organizers speak the presentation. They are easy to do, inexpensive and accomplish many of our persuasion and social media goals at one time.

As with every other form of content, in order to be effective they must be done correctly. By webinar I do not mean having someone, reading slides and just going on and on and on about their product and company. Not to say once someone has purchased a product a webinar explaining every detail is bad, that is awesome and will probably cut down on buyer's remorse and increase the productivity generated by your product, since the buyer will have a better understanding on how to use all the product benefits.

What I am describing is the best way (along with books) to present your company as the Industry Expert. By offering useful information in an interactive environment your prospects will get to know you, be grateful and want to learn more from you. A major part of the puzzle is to give a lot of overall industry information and not promoting your product the whole time.

Depending on your desired outcome, whether it be a sale, introduction to your company, just plain great information, there are well defined guidelines for creating and implementing webinars..

Webinars are a great way to qualify your leads. This can be done by monitoring questions, length of time prospects stays on the webinar, if prospect takes action on the next step recommended in the webinar. Out and out asking where the prospect is in the buying decision can be easily accomplished. Below is a sample from one of my webinars, the prospect is asked to choose which describes them best:

⚔ When can we get my books started

⚔ I love it, just need to fill in the dots

- I need to get my management team involved

- Interesting, I would like to learn more

- No thanks, but I will keep it in mind

- No thanks

With automation tools, webinars can be offered several times a day every day of the week, still be interactive and appear as if they were live. One of the major hurdles to successfully selling a large company is having the prospect make your presentation to their manager. Yet with a webinar the prospect will receive a replay link afterward and can then have their manager watch your presentation instead of trying to paraphrase what he or she remembers from the presentation.

Think of the advantages your salesperson will have when they contact the prospect who already has a basic idea about your product and why they need it. The salesperson is also able to prepare ahead knowing what questions the prospect asked during the webinar.

If you are trying to sell a product via the webinar, industry averages for a sales letter on the internet are 1% to 2% while webinar sales are over 10%.

Webinar benefits include:

- Drastic Reduction is Sales Process Investment

- Increase in speed of Sales Process

- Able to generate multiple sales at once

Tips on creating a webinar

- Brief bio of presents
- Create an open loop that will be answered at end of presentation

- Give a Bonus at the end of webinar for those who stay to end
- Q & A based on your company's biggest objections
- Break up flow every 7 to 8 minutes (Keep viewers attention from wandering)
- If trying to sell at add bonuses for purchasing with perceived value more than product
- Add some fun to it
- Make some simple mistakes to make presenter more real and likable
- Give actionable information if possible

Other types of communications that should be included in every follow up but are pretty self-explanatory include:

- ⋏ Newsletter
- ⋏ Blog Posts
- ⋏ Flashdrives
- ⋏ Your Social Media Sites
- ⋏ Phone Calls

Conclusion

Thank you for taking this journey with me. Many times I have heard of the internet described as the Wild Wild West. I guess in many ways that may be true. Certainly the pure wonder of it's potential is awe inspiring. Yet at the same time there are many dangers hiding beyond the next curve in the road.

Blindly heading down a new path may be exhilarating, yet also full of risks. Though out the book I have quoted from many experts on proven strategies for success. There is no reason just because the internet is new and ever changing to ignore sound business principles.

My hopes for you are that you take a serious look at the path I have described and use it to your company's utmost benefit. Experiment, use what works for your company and discard the rest. Take action, create an Industry Expert Status for your company and reap the rewards.

The greatest reward being the ability to put the Fun back in growing your business.

To your Expert Status

Jeff Grundy

Thank you for your time and I truly wish you the best of success in converting your sales into leads.
For more information on putting the fun back into growing your business, contact:

866-337-6188
http://www.TradeShowROI.org

Text TradeShow to 71441
To experience Trade Show ROI 26 week follow up sequence for yourself

www.ingramcontent.com/pod-product-compliance
Lightning Source LLC
Chambersburg PA
CBHW051319170526
45166CB00002B/605